Memorabilia Quilts

Fabulous Projects with Keepsakes & Collectibles

Linda Causee
Rita Weiss

Sterling Publishing Co., Inc.
New York

Produced by: The Creative Partners,™LLC
Book Design: Joyce Lerner
Photography: Carol Wilson Mansfield
Technical Editing: Ann Harnden

Special Thanks to:
Faith Horsky
who quilted many of the quilts

Fairfield Processing Corportion:
Machine 60/40 Blend® Batting

Library of Congress Cataloging-in-Publication Data Available

10 9 8 7 6 5 4 3 2 1

Published by Sterling Publishing Co., Inc.
387 Park Avenue South, New York, NY 10016
© 2007 by The Creative Partners™ LLC
Distributed in Canada by Sterling Publishing
c/o Canadian Manda Group, 165 Dufferin Street,
Toronto, Ontario, Canada M6K 3H6
Distributed in the United Kingdom by GMC Distribution Services,
Castle Place, 166 High Street, Lewes, East Sussex, England BN7 1XU
Distributed in Australia by Capricorn Link (Australia) Pty. Ltd.
P.O. Box 704, Windsor, NSW 2756, Australia

Sterling ISBN-13-978-1-4027-3353-6
       ISBN-10: 1-4027-3353-4

For information about custom editions, special sales, premium and
corporate purchases, please contact Sterling Special Sales
Department at 800-805-5489 or specialsales@sterlingpub.com.

Introduction

What can you do with
all of the bits and pieces
you have collected in
your life?

Does your son's T-shirt collection
take up space in your house long after he's left home?
Where are the blue ribbons you won at the State Fair
or the pins from your favorite baseball team? Where
are your prized family photos?

If you could make a time capsule of those precious
moments in your life, what would you put into it?
Bits and pieces saved? Pictures of your family? Your
grandmother's crocheted handkerchiefs? Notes from
your children? Postcards? How best to savor them
through the years?

Have you ever thought of enshrining those precious
moments into wonderful quilts that could hang on your
wall or be used to keep you warm? Why not make a
quilt from the ties your father wore during his working
years? How about taking your son's T-shirt collection
and turning it into a quilt for his bed? Did you save
those ticket stubs to remind you of the concerts you
attended? Put them together into a musical quilt.
Instead of keeping picture postcards in the drawer, copy
them onto fabric and make a quilt. How about a quilt to
commemorate a wedding or an important anniversary?

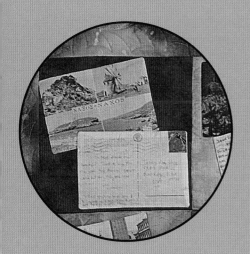

We both love to do just that—make quilts to
keep our memories alive. We're delighted to
share these quilts with you in this book, and
we hope that they will inspire you to create
quilts with your own memorabilia.

Linda Causee   *Rita Weiss*

Contents

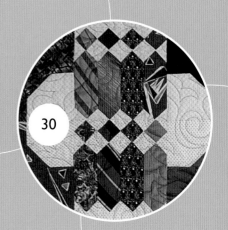

36

62

88

Sunday
April 30, 1978
Fall Brook Theatre
3:30 PM

42

68

92

48

72

98

Concert Hall

Aspen
Music Festival
cital with Mitsuko Uchida

Harris Concert Hall
Aug 07, 1996 8:00 PM
tr   Row C   Seat 20
FP $24.00(M)

54

76

104

MCJROTC

OCEANSIDE C

Ports of Call

by Linda Causee

When my son, Chris, was commissioned as an Ensign in the US Navy and started on his big adventure, I knew I wanted to make something to commemorate this experience.

I began collecting all the memorabilia that he sent home from his port stops. Because I tend to think of everything in terms of a quilt, I decided to make a series of small quilts focusing on one experience. Each little quilt contains an outline map of the location with pictures, postcards and even some of the currency that he had sent home.

The quilt series began in California where he was commissioned and moved to his duty stations in Sasebo, Japan and Norfolk, Virginia. It commemorated two deployments to the Persian Gulf and port stops in Singapore, Thailand, United Arab Emerites, Bahrain, Monaco, Italy, Croatia, Greece, and The Seychelles. Included was a tangle with pirates off the coast of Somalia and several shorter trips to ports in Australia, South Korea, Hong Kong, Philippines and Guam.

In three years, I had more than 15 little quilts and little room to display them. I decided it would be fun to join all of the little quilts into one large wall hanging. There were many ways to connect the little quilts, but I preferred to use rope tied in nautical knots in keeping with the naval theme. The little quilts were placed five across and four down, leaving one extra space for the next adventure.

He is planning to make the Navy his career. I can, therefore, look forward to many additions to this quilt and following him wherever the Navy takes him.

Do you have an adventurer in your life?

—Linda Causee

Ports of Call

Approximate Size: 45" x 48"

Materials

Note: *Fabric amounts will make up to 20 small quilts.*
2 yards navy blue print (background)
1/2 yard green (countries)
1/2 yard beige (countries)
1/2 yard beige/gray (countries)
1/8 yard white (lettering)
2 yards backing
thin batting
*prepared fabric sheets
    (You will need 1-2 sheets per small quilt)
paper-backed fusible web
tracing paper
black felt tip pen
quilting (or thick) thread, rope, buttons, grommets,
    ribbon, yarn, etc. (to attached small quilts together)
maps of various countries
assorted photos and postcards

   Purchase prepared fabric sheets or refer to Preparing Your Own Fabric for Printing, page 121, to make your own.

Cutting

Cut the following for each small quilt:
1 rectangle, 9 1/2" x 12 1/2", navy blue print
1 rectangle, 9 1/2" x 12 1/2", backing
1 rectangle, 9 1/2" x 12 1/2", batting

Instructions

Small Quilts

1. Find outline maps of countries visited via the internet, encyclopedias, atlases, etc. If the map is either too large or too small to fit onto the 9 1/2" x 12 1/2" background, you will need to adjust the size by using a copier. Try to make the length no more than 6" and the width no more than 4" to allow room for assorted photos.

2. Once your map is the correct size, trace onto tracing paper using a black felt tip pen. Turn traced map over so that it is backwards, then trace flopped map onto paper side of fusible web. **Note:** *You must trace flopped map onto paper-backed fusible web for your resulting image to be correct.* (**Diagram 1**)

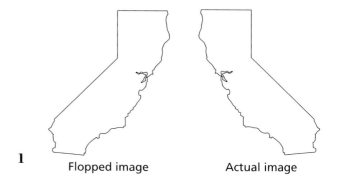

1   Flopped image   Actual image

3. Iron fusible web on onto wrong side of green, beige or beige/gray fabric following manufacturer's directions. Cut out along drawn line. (**Diagram 2**)

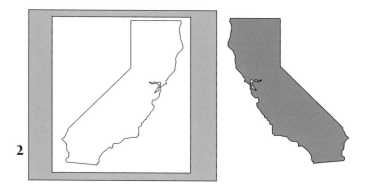

2

4. Re-size photos so that they are about 2" x 3" or 3" x 4" and print onto prepared fabric sheets referring to Printing Photos to Fabric, pages 121 to 122.

5. Print the name of the country onto fabric. Use your computer to type the country's name and then print onto fabric using your printer or hand write them directly onto

white fabric. Iron paper-backed fusible web to back of country's name and trim fabric about 1/2" from name all around. (**Diagram 3**)

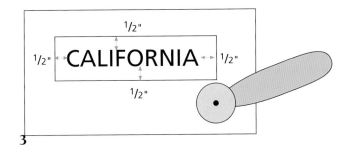

3

6. Position country name onto background rectangle about 1" from top edge. Next, place country underneath name and finally place photos and postcards around country. Fuse in place. (**Diagram 4**)

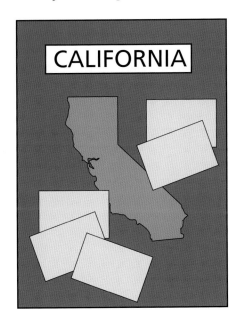

4

7. Place the finished top right sides together with the backing rectangle. Place batting rectangle underneath. Sew along all four sides using a 1/4" seam allowance, leaving a 4" opening along one side. (**Diagram 5**) Turn small quilt right side out through opening. Sew opening closed.

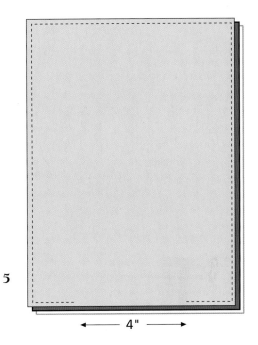

5

←——— 4" ———→

8. Repeat steps 1 to 7 for remaining countries.

9. Topstitch 1/4" from edge of small quilts. Stitch along edges of countries, photos and country name if desired.

10. Use matching thread and stitch small quilts together in rows at corners. (**Diagram 6**) Then stitch rows together at corners. (**Diagram 7**)

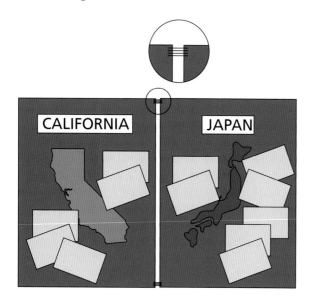

6

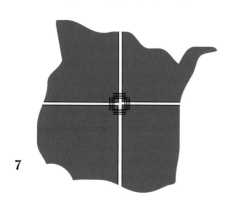

7

11. To cover stitches, use nautical knots. Cut thin rope into 12" lengths. Tie rope into a Triple Overhand Knot (**Diagram 8**); cut ends to 1". Attach a knot to upper and lower corners, tucking ends under and covering previous stitching.

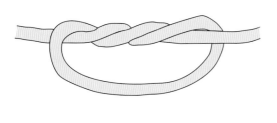

8

Other Options:

1. Sew a button where four corners meet to cover stitching. (**Diagram 9**)

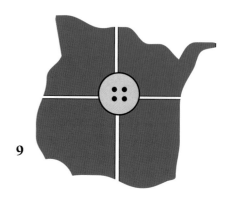

9

2. Place a grommet in each corner of each small quilt following directions on package. Thread string, ribbon or yarn through grommets and tie into knots or bows. (**Diagram 10**)

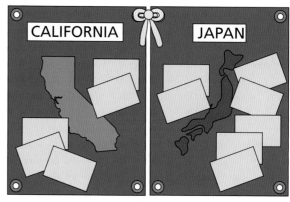

10

"Because I tend to think of everything in terms of a quilt, I decided to make a series of small quilts focusing on one experience."

Ports of Call Quilt Layout

Our Family Photo Album

by Rita Weiss

My mother-in-law, Kate, loved posing for photos, and she loved collecting the photos for which her family posed. Each photo was carefully mounted in a photo album. Black hinges served to hold the photo on the album's black pages.

My husband, her only child, inherited her photo albums, and we spent many warm hours pouring over these old photos. I loved the way each photo was so tastefully arranged on the pages. I always hesitated to remove any picture to place in a frame because we were so concerned that an old photo in a frame could disintegrate unless it were archivally preserved. But preserving one photo at a time meant we could look at only one photo. And, we would miss the charming view of the album.

This quilt is my solution. Eleven old family photos are presented as if they were pages from the family photo album. The remainder of Kate's collection are just waiting to be made into additional quilts. Now Kate's descendents—including the youngest Kate recently born—can enjoy the photos.

I think she would approve.

—Rita Weiss

Our Family Photo Album

Approximate Size: 40" x 36"

Materials

1 1/2 yards black (includes border and binding)
3/4 yard beige old-fashioned print
*prepared fabric sheets
11 photos
backing
1 1/4 yards backing
craft-size batting
1 yard lightweight paper-backed fusible web
pinking sheers or rotary cutter with pinking blade
   *Purchase prepared fabric sheets or refer to Preparing Your
   Own Fabric for Printing, page 121, to make your own.

Cutting

Blocks

7 rectangles, 8 1/2" x 10 1/2", black
2 rectangles, 7 1/2" x 8 1/2", black

Finishing

13 strips, 1 1/2"-wide, beige old-fashioned print (frames)
4 strips, 3 1/2"-wide, black (border)
4 strips, 2 1/2"-wide, black (binding)

Instructions

1. Referring to Printing Photos to Fabric, pages 121 to 122, print photos to fabric, re-sizing photos to fit within the 8" x 10" or 7" x 8" finished black rectangles.

2. Trim photos about 1/2" from all edges, then fuse onto paper-backed fusible web. Using pinking sheers or a rotary cutter with a pinking blade, trim photos about 1/4" from edge of photo. (**Diagram 1**)

1

3. Referring to photograph on page 12 as a guide, arrange photos on black rectangles. If photos are small, place two on one black rectangle. Fuse in place.

4. Fuse a piece of black fabric (at least 5" x 5") to paper-backed fusible web. Cut out 22 one-inch squares; cut squares in half diagonally. Fuse a triangle to each corner of each photo.

5. Sew around edges of photos using a small machine zigzag stitch and invisible thread.

6. Place a black photo rectangle right sides together with 1 1/2" beige print strip. Sew using a 1/4" seam allowance. Press strip open and trim strip even with edge of black rectangle. (**Diagram 2**)

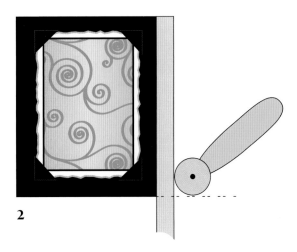

2

7. Turn black rectangle counterclockwise, place beige print strip right sides together with black rectangle along right edge. Sew, fold strip open and trim strip even with black rectangle. (**Diagram 3**)

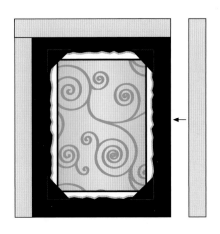

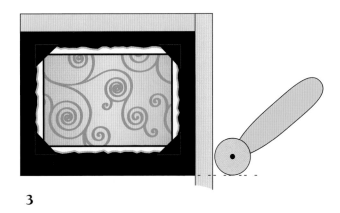

3

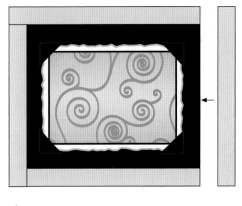

4

8. Repeat steps 6 and 7 for remaining two sides. (**Diagram 4**)

9. Repeat steps 6 to 8 for remaining black photo rectangles.

10. Sew framed rectangles together in vertical rows, then sew rows together. (**Diagram 5**)

11. Measure quilt lengthwise. Cut two 3½" black strips to that length and sew to sides of quilt. Measure quilt crosswise. Cut two 3½" black strips to that length and sew to top and bottom of quilt.

12. Refer to Finishing Your Quilt, page 123 to 127, to complete your quilt.

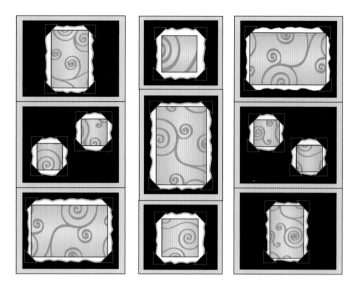

5

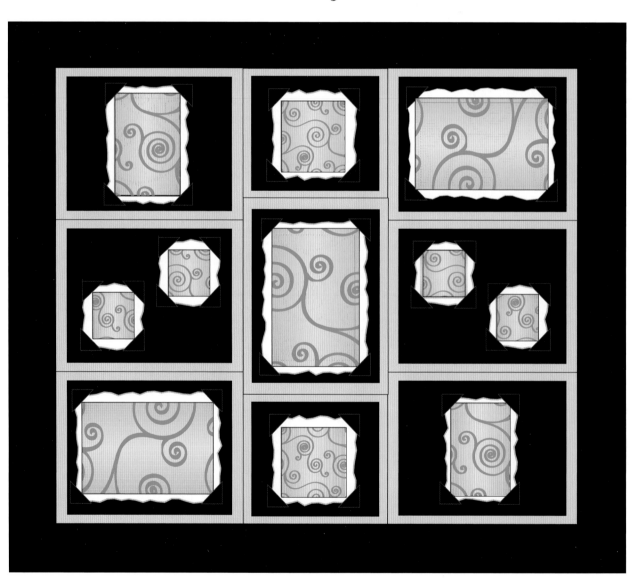

Photo Scrapbook Quilt Layout

"Now Kate's descendents—
including the youngest Kate
recently born—can enjoy
the photos. I think she would
approve."

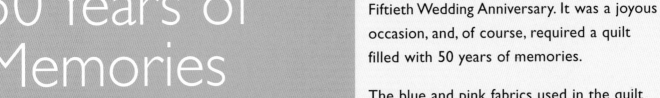

50 Years of Memories

by Linda Causee

It was time to celebrate my parents' Fiftieth Wedding Anniversary. It was a joyous occasion, and, of course, required a quilt filled with 50 years of memories.

The blue and pink fabrics used in the quilt represent the colors worn by the original wedding party. The hearts scattered through the quilt symbolize their love, for each other and for their family.

Their anniversary photo is framed in gold in the center, and they are surrounded by pictures of their three children and grand-children. At the top of the quilt, I placed a picture of the happy couple heading off 50 years ago for the big adventure.

The quilt itself has now become a family heirloom to be handed down to future generations. How much better than a bunch of photos sleeping in a drawer!

—*Linda Causee*

50 Years of Memories

Approximate Size: 36" x 36"

Materials

9 large photos (to finish 6" x 6")
12-16 photos (to finish 3" x 3")
*prepared fabric sheets
1 1/2 yards gold fabric (includes border and binding)
1/2 yard pink
5/8 yard blue print
1/2 yard blue floral print
1 1/4 yards backing
batting

 *Purchase prepared fabric sheets or refer to Preparing Your
 Own Fabric for Printing, page 121, to make your own.

Pattern (page 23)

Heart Foundation

Cutting

Picture Frames

18 strips, 1 1/2" x 6 1/2", gold
18 strips, 1 1/2" x 8 1/2", gold
24-32 strips, 1" x 3 1/2", gold
24-32 strips, 1" x 4 1/2", gold

Hearts

Note: *Although you do not have to cut exact pieces for
foundation piecing, you may cut the following pieces to make
the heart blocks.*
12 squares, 4 1/2" x 4 1/2", pink (space 4)
2 strips, 1"-wide, pink (spaces 1 and 3)
12 squares, 3" x 3", blue print
 (cut in half diagonally, spaces 7 and 8)
1 strip, 1 1/2"-wide, blue print (space 2)
12 squares, 2" x 2", blue print
 (cut in half diagonally, spaces 5 and 6)

Finishing

4 strips, 2 1/2"-wide, blue floral (first border)
4 strips, 4 1/2"-wide, gold (second border)
4 strips, 2 1/2"-wide, gold (binding)

Instructions

Note: *Refer to Printing Photos to Fabric, pages 121 to 122, to
transfer your photos to fabric.*

1. Adjust photos so that they will finish as 6" and 3"
squares, then print or copy onto prepared fabric sheets.
Trim large photos to 6 1/2" x 6 1/2" and small photos to
3 1/2" x 3 1/2".

2. For 6 1/2" photos, sew 1 1/2" x 6 1/2" gold strips to opposite sides of photo. Sew 1 1/2" x 8 1/2" gold strips to top
and bottom. Repeat for all photos. (**Diagram 1**)

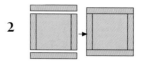

3. For 3 1/2" photos, sew 1" x 3 1/2" gold strips to opposite
sides of photos. Sew 1" x 4 1/2" gold strips to top and bottom. (**Diagram 2**)

4. For Hearts, refer to Preparing the Foundation, pages
114 to 115, to make 16 foundations using pattern on page
23. (**Diagram 3**)

5. Refer to Foundation Piecing, pages 114 to 119, to
make 16 Heart blocks. (**Diagram 4**)

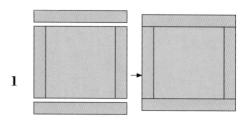

6. Sew a small framed photo to a heart; repeat switching placement of photo and heart. (**Diagram 5**)

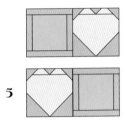

4. Sew two small photo blocks together horizontally; sew small heart block to each end. (**Diagram 9**) Repeat.

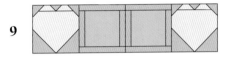

7. Sew together units from step 6 to make a Four Patch. (**Diagram 6**)

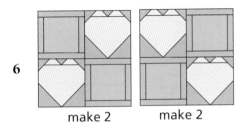

make 2   make 2

8. Repeat steps 6 and 7 for three more Four Patches. Note opposite placement for two of the Four Patches.

Finishing

1. Lay out blocks to decide on placement of photos.

2. Sew two small photo blocks together vertically. (**Diagram 7**) Repeat.

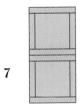

3. Sew photo pairs to opposite sides of photo chosen for center of quilt. (**Diagram 8**)

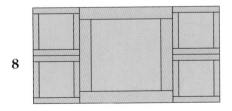

5. Sew to top and bottom of unit from step 3. (**Diagram 10**)

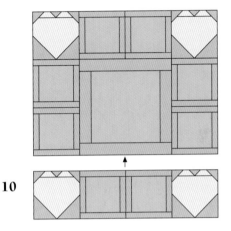

6. Sew two large photos vertically. (**Diagram 11**) Repeat.

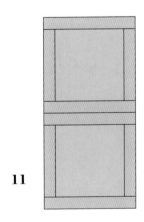

7. Sew vertical pairs of photos to sides of center photo. (**Diagram 12**)

8. Sew two large photos together horizontally; sew a Four Patch from step 8 to each end. Repeat noting position of Four Patches. (**Diagram 13**)

9. Sew to top and bottom of quilt. (**Diagram 14**)

10. Measure quilt lengthwise. Sew 2$\frac{1}{2}$" blue floral strips to opposite sides. Measure quilt crosswise. Sew 2$\frac{1}{2}$" blue floral strips to top and bottom. Repeat for 4$\frac{1}{2}$" gold border strips.

12. Refer to Finishing Your Quilt, pages 123 to 127, to complete quilt.
Note: *Do not quilt through photos.*

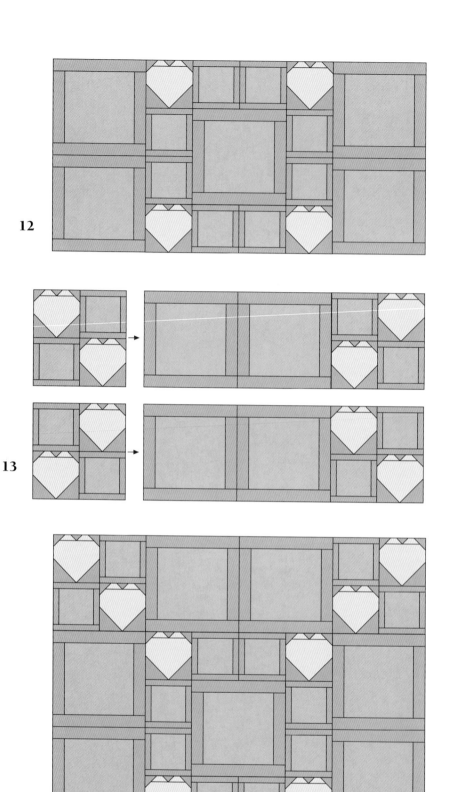

12

13

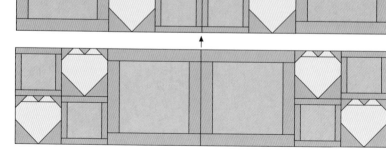

14

50 Years of Memories Quilt Layout

"The blue and pink fabrics used in the quilt represent the colors worn by the original wedding party. The hearts scattered through the quilt symbolize their love, for each other and for their family."

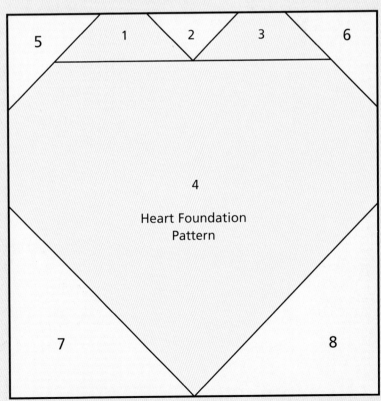

Heart Foundation Pattern

50 Years of Memories Pattern Piece

Postcards From....

by Rita Weiss

"Send me a picture postcard from an exotic place, and I'll save it forever."

That has always been my mantra. What did I ever expect to do with those postcards? I'm not sure. Take them out of the shoe box I'm saving them in and enjoy the scenery? Probably never. Reread the message on the back? I've probably forgot the sender.

So why do I save postcards? Probably because they are too pretty to throw away and probably because they call attention to places I might want to someday visit.

There is a batch of postcards, however, that have had a special place in my collection: the postcards sent to me by my daughter, Michelle, when she traveled through Europe in her junior year. Rather than have these precious mementos sleeping in a musty shoe box, I kept looking for a way to capture them in such a way as to make them a part of everyday life.

Once I became a quilter, the answer was a simple one. Put the postcards into a quilt. Display the fronts and the backs of the cards so I could not only see the wonderful spots she visited, but also read her messages, still fresh after so many years. And, in the center of the quilt, I've placed a replica of the mailbox that held those cards upon their arrival. Now, whenever I look up from my desk, the postcards and the messages are still there.

I haven't destroyed any of the original postcards. They're still in their special shoe box.

-Rita Weiss

Postcards From....

Approximate Size: 27" x 27"

Materials

fat quarter red
fat quarter yellow
fat quarter green
fat quarter purple
1 yard blue (includes border and binding)
scrap brown
7/8 yard backing
batting
8 postcards
*9 prepared fabric sheets
1 sheet of copy paper (for foundation piecing)
  *Purchase prepared fabric sheets or refer to Preparing Fabric
  for Printing, page 119, to make your own.

Pattern (page 28)

Mailbox Foundation

Cutting

2 squares, 7 1/2" x 7 1/2", red
2 squares, 7 1/2" x 7 1/2", yellow
2 squares, 7 1/2" x 7 1/2", green
2 squares, 7 1/2" x 7 1/2", purple
2 strips, 3 1/2" x 21 1/2", blue (side border)
2 strips, 3 1/2" x 27 1/2", blue (top and bottom border)
3 strips, 2 1/2"-wide, blue (binding)

Instructions

1. Referring to Printing Photos to Fabric, pages 121 to 122, print the front and back of each postcard.
Hint: *Print two fronts or two backs per fabric sheet.*

2. Arrange the front and back of a postcard on the right side of a 7 1/2" fabric square. Referring to Easy Appliqué, pages 119-120, and using a machine zigzag stitch, appliqué postcards in place. (**Diagram 1**) Repeat for remaining seven blocks.

1

3. Referring to Foundation Piecing, pages 114 to 119, prepare a foundation and piece the Mailbox block. (**Diagram 2**)

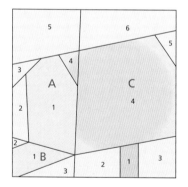
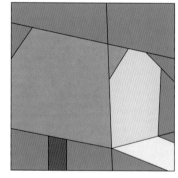

2

4. Arrange Postcard blocks around Mailbox block in three rows of three blocks. Sew blocks together in rows, then sew rows together. (**Diagram 3**)

5. Sew 3¹/2" x 21¹/2" blue strip to sides of quilt. Press seams toward border. Sew 3¹/2" x 27¹/2" blue strip to top and bottom of quilt. Press seams toward border.

6. Refer to Finishing Your Quilt, pages 123 to 127, to complete your quilt.

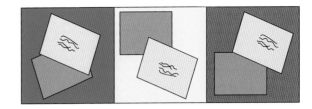

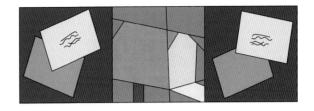

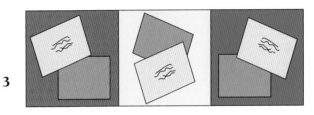

3

Postcards From....
Quilt Layout

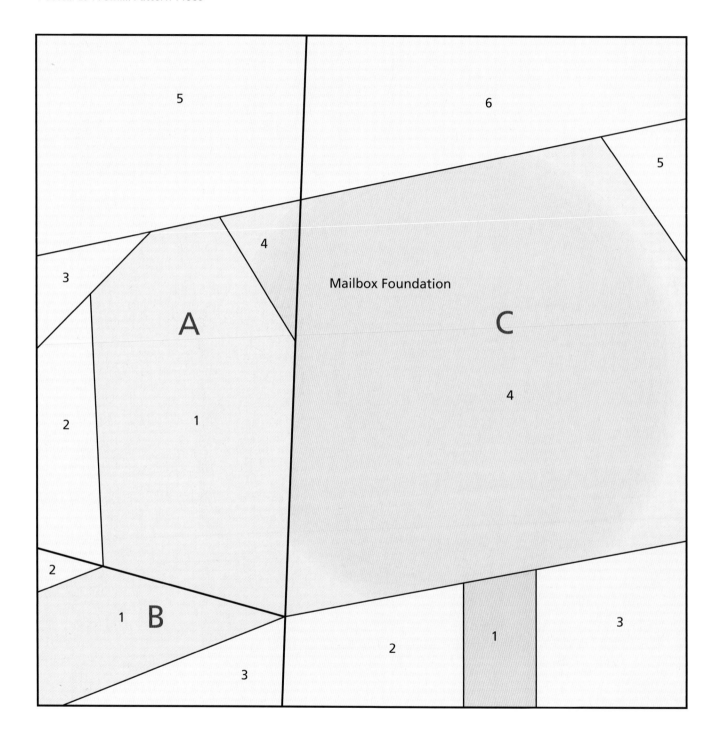

"Send me a picture postcard from an exotic place, and I'll save it forever."

"...I kept looking for a way to capture them in such a way as to make them a part of every day life."

My Father's Ties

by Linda Causee

When I was a child, my father went to work every day dressed in a business suit, a shirt and a tie. I loved those ties because they added such a bright note of color.

When my father retired, he took off his tie and vowed that he would never wear a tie again. What I had considered bright and colorful, he had considered a chain that kept him tied to a desk. Now he was going to do all the things he wanted to do, and that did not include wearing a tie!

He would have thrown away the ties, but I rescued them because I loved their cheery colors, and they reminded me of my own youth and my father. Rather than keep the ties bundled in a drawer, I decided to put them together into a quilt. I recreated miniature ties for some of the blocks, and I used the Bow Tie block for the others. The tiny prints that are used for the background look like some of dad's old shirts.

Now whenever I look at this quilt, I will always be reminded of my father. When he saw the quilt, he exclaimed, "If I'd known you could make something this pretty, I would have worn more ties!"

—*Linda Causee*

My Father's Ties

Approximate Size: 55" x 55"
Block Size: 8" x 8" finished

Materials

16-20 men's ties (One tie will make 3-4
    small ties for blocks)
1/2 yard each of four different light prints
11/2 yards dark print (border and binding)
3 yards backing
twin-size batting
5 yards lightweight fusible interfacing

Cutting

Note: *Carefully open seam at back of each tie and press to remove folds. Following manufacturer's directions, iron fusible interfacing to wrong side of pressed ties. Cut squares and strips from the tie fabric.*

Tie Blocks

64 strips, 21/2" x 61/2", tie fabric
64 squares, 21/2" x 21/2", tie fabric
512 squares, 11/2" x 11/2", light background prints
    (128 from each light print)

Bow Tie Blocks

32 squares, 41/2" x 41/2", light background prints
    (8 from each print)
32 squares, 41/2" x 41/2", tie fabric
32 squares, 21/2" x 21/2", tie fabric

Plain Blocks

4 squares, 81/2" x 81/2", light background
    (1 from each light background print)

Finishing

6 strips, 4"-wide, dark print (border)
6 strips, 21/2"-wide, dark print (binding)

Instructions

Note: *Use the same tie fabric for rectangle and square in steps 1 and 2.*

Tie Blocks

1. Using the Stitch and Flip method, page 113, sew 11/2" background squares diagonally to corners of 21/2" x 61/2" tie rectangle. Trim 1/4" from seam and flip back resulting triangles. (**Diagram 1**)

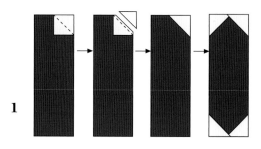

2. Sew 11/2" background squares diagonally to 21/2" tie square; trim 1/4" from seams and flip each resulting triangle. (**Diagram 2**)

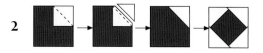

3. Sew the pieced rectangle and square together to complete a tie. (**Diagram 3**)

4. Repeat steps 1 to 3 to make remaining 63 ties.

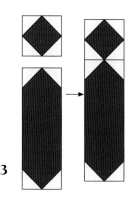

5. Sew four ties together to complete Tie block. (**Diagram 4**) Make 16 Tie Blocks.

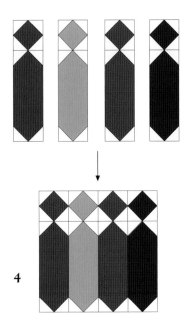

4

2. Sew background/triangle square to 4¹/2" tie print square. (**Diagram 6**) Repeat.

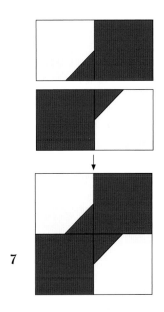

6

3. Sew pair of squares together to complete Bow Tie block. (**Diagram 7**) Make a total of 16 Bow Tie blocks.

7

Bow Tie Blocks

Note: *Work with same tie print for a single block.*

1. Sew a 2¹/2" tie print square to one corner of a 4¹/2" background square. Trim ¹/4" from seam and flip back resulting triangle. (**Diagram 5**) Repeat.

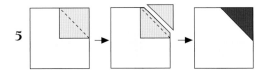

5

Finishing

Note: *The quilt is made up of four sections each with a different light background print.*

1. For row 2, sew a Tie Block to opposite sides of an 8¹/₂" print square. For rows 1 and 3, sew Bow Tie Block to opposite sides of Tie Block; repeat. (**Diagram 8**)

8

2. Sew rows together to complete one section of the quilt. (**Diagram 9**)

9

3. Repeat steps 1 and 2 for remaining three sections.

4. Sew sections in pairs, then sew pairs together. (**Diagram 10**)

5. Measure quilt lengthwise. Piece and cut two 4"-wide dark print strips to that length; sew to sides of quilt. Measure quilt crosswise. Piece and cut two 4"-wide dark print strips to that length; sew to top and bottom of quilt.

6. Refer to Finishing Your Quilt, pages 123 to 127, to complete quilt.

10

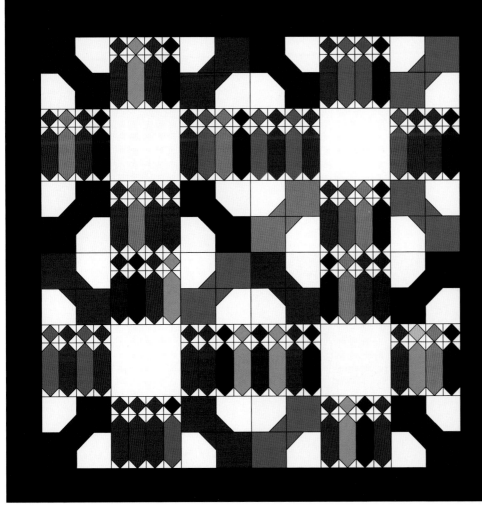

"If I'd known you could make something this pretty, I would have worn more ties!"

My Father's Ties
Quilt Layout

My Trophy Case

by Rita Weiss

If you like to enter competitions whether it's cake decorating or quilt shows, you may have amassed a collection of ribbons.

I know all about ribbons because when my children were young, the entire family was immersed in raising and showing dogs. We loved the various color ribbons, each one representing a special award for a special dog. The kids loved the bright-color ribbons; even the dogs could be more enthusiastic over a blue ribbon (first place) as opposed to a red ribbon (second place).

In addition to ribbons, we also collected trophies. There was never a problem as to where to put the trophies; they could go into a trophy case that hung on the wall, but what to do with the ribbons? Once you give up dog showing for quilt making, the answer is obvious. You make a quilted showcase for your ribbons.

After you have completed the showcase quilt, you can arrange the ribbon display as you wish, adding the latest awards or keeping some of your favorite old ones. Photos of the winning peach pie, the blue ribbon knitted sweater or the spectacular quilt can be attached to the "shelves."

Now you can be a real prize winner!

—Rita Weiss

My Trophy Case

Approximate Size: 52" x 62"

Materials

1³/4 yards solid black fabric

⁵/8 yard light brown

1¹/2 yards dark brown (includes border and binding)

thin batting

*prepared fabric sheets (Use 1 fabric sheet per photo)

ribbons and photos

*Purchase prepared fabric sheets or refer to Preparing Your
Own Fabric for Printing, page 121, to make your own.

Cutting

Blocks

8 squares, 9¹/2" x 9¹/2", black

4 rectangles, 9¹/2" x 12¹/2", black

1 rectangle, 20¹/2" x 26¹/2", black

12 strips, 2¹/2" x 11⁷/8", dark brown

1 strip, 2¹/2" x 22⁷/8", dark brown

8 strips, 2¹/2" x 11⁷/8", light brown

4 strips, 2¹/2" x 14⁷/8", light brown

1 strip, 2¹/2" x 28⁷/8", light brown

Finishing

6 strips, 2¹/2"-wide, dark brown (border)

6 strips, 2¹/2"-wide, dark brown (binding)

Instructions

Large Rectangle A (make 1)

1. Place 2¹/2" x 28⁷/8" light brown strip right sides together with 20¹/2" x 26¹/2" black rectangle along long left edge. Upper edge of light brown strip will extend past the upper edge of the black rectangle. (**Diagram 1**)

1

2. Beginning at top edge, sew with a ¹/4" seam allowance to within ¹/4" from bottom edge of black rectangle. (**Diagram 2**)

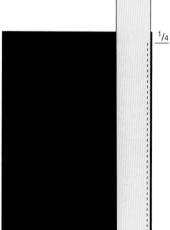

¹/4"

2

3. Place 2¹/2" x 22⁷/8" dark brown strip right sides together with upper edge of black rectangle; be sure that extended end is at same corner with light brown strip. (**Diagram 3**)

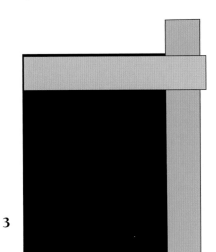

5. Place extended ends of light brown and dark brown strips together. Draw a 45 degree diagonal line from stitching toward outside edge. (**Diagram 5**)

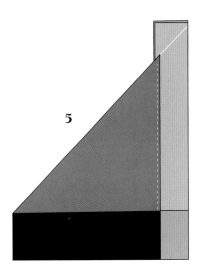

4. Beginning at even edges, sew with a ¹/4" seam allowance to seamline of dark brown strip and black rectangle. (**Diagram 4**)

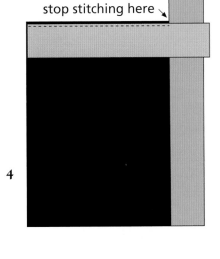

6. Sew along drawn line starting at corner and sewing toward outer edge. (**Diagram 6**)

7. Trim fabric ¹/4" from sewn line. (**Diagram 7**)

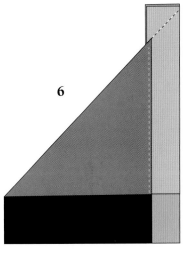

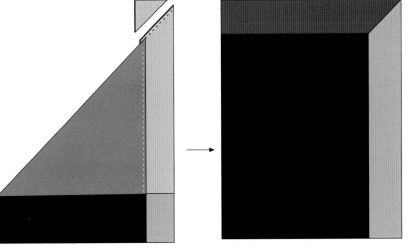

Small Rectangle B (make 4)

1. Repeat steps 1 to 7 for 9¹/2" x 12¹/2" black rectangles and 2¹/2" x 14⁷/8" light brown and 2¹/2" x 71⁷/8"dark brown strips. (**Diagram 8**)

8

Square C (make 8)

1. Repeat steps 1 to 7 for 9¹/2" x 9¹/2" black squares and 2¹/2" x 11⁷/8" light brown and dark brown strips. (**Diagram 9**)

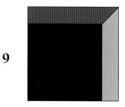

9

Finishing

1. Sew two Small Rectangle B together along short edge; repeat. (**Diagram 10**)

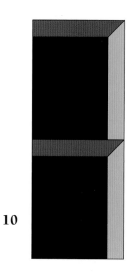

10

2. Sew Small Rectangle pairs to opposite sides of Large Rectangle A. (**Diagram 11**)

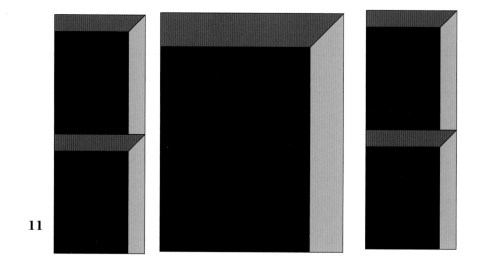

11

3. Sew four Square C together; repeat. (**Diagram 12**)

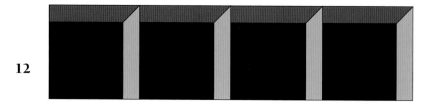

12

4. Sew rows of Squares to top and bottom of Rectangle section. (**Diagram 13**)

5. Measure quilt top lengthwise; sew and cut two 2¹/2"-wide dark brown strips to opposite sides of quilt. Measure quilt top crosswise; sew and cut two 2¹/2"-wide dark brown strips to top and bottom of quilt top.

6. Refer to Finishing Your Quilt, pages 123 to 127, to complete your quilt.

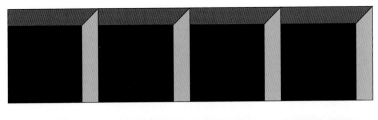

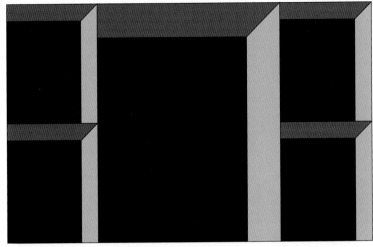

13

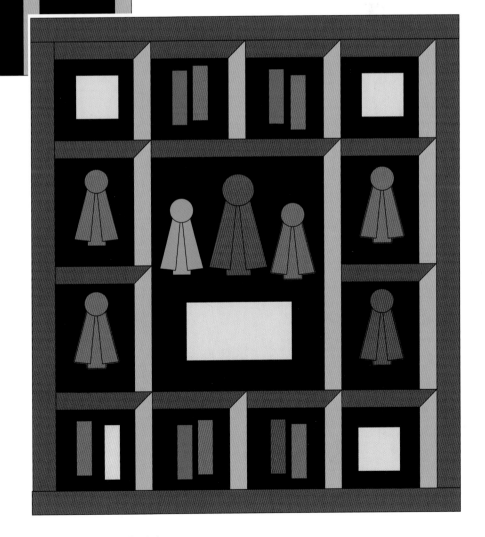

"Once you give up dog
showing for quilt making,
the answer is obvious.
You make a quilted show-
case for your ribbons."

Finishing

1. Attach ribbons by hand stitching to
black areas of quilt.

2. Print photos on prepared fabric
sheets, referring to Printing Photos to
Fabric, pages 121 to 122.

3. Attach photos to black areas of quilt
referring to Appliqué with Fusible
Interfacing, pages 119 to 120.

My Trophy Case Quilt Layout

High School Memories

by Linda Causee

When my daughter graduated from high school, knowing how interested I was in memorabilia quilts, she asked me if I would make a quilt of her high school memories.

We decided that the quilt would contain the signatures of her friends along with photos of their school life together. We began by giving each friend a square of fabric, which was signed with a permanent marking pen. The signature squares were then made into quilt squares by bordering them with the school colors of brown and gold.

After the entire quilt top was completed, the borders provided the perfect spot to place the pictures. We chose those photos that best captured high school life and the memories she most wanted to keep.

The quilt now not only keeps her warm as a cover for her bed, but also always reminds her of warm friendships and the friends she doesn't want to lose.

—Linda Causee

High School Memories

Approximate Size: 66" x 66"
Block Size: 9" x 9" finished

Materials

2¹/2 yards yard ecru
*1 yard gold
*1 yard brown
2¹/4 yards brown (border and binding)
4 yards backing
batting
permanent fabric markers
**prepared fabric sheets and assorted photos
  *Photographed quilt uses assorted brown and gold prints
  totaling the amounts given.
  **Purchase prepared fabric sheets or make your own
  referring to Preparing Your Own Fabric for Printing,
  page 121.

Cutting

Blocks

36 rectangles, 3¹/2" x 6¹/2", ecru
72 rectangles, 2" x 3¹/2", ecru
8 strips, 3¹/2"-wide, ecru
8 strips, 2"-wide, ecru
12 strips, 2"-wide, gold
12 strips, 2"-wide, brown

Finishing

8 strips, 6¹/2"-wide, brown (brown)
8 strips, 2¹/2"-wide, brown (binding)

Instructions

Blocks

1. Sew 3¹/2" ecru strip to 2"-wide brown strip; press seam
toward brown. Repeat for three more strip sets.
(**Diagram 1**)

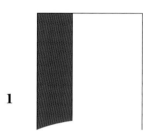

2. Cut strip sets at 2" intervals for 72 Unit A. (**Diagram 2**)

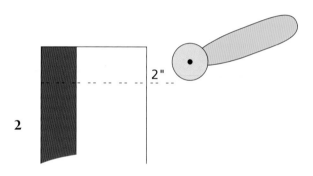

3. Repeat steps 1 and 2 using 3¹/2" ecru strips and 2" gold
strips for 72 Unit B. (**Diagram 3**)

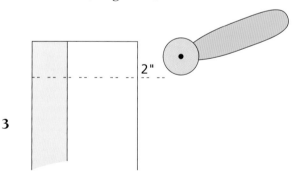

4. Sew 2" gold and 2" brown strips together. Repeat for three more strip sets. (**Diagram 4**)

4

5. Cut strip sets at 2" intervals for 72 Unit C. (**Diagram 5**)

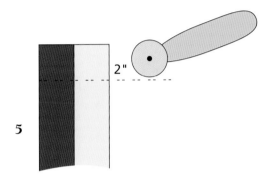

2"

5

6. Repeat steps 4 and 5 using 2" ecru strips and 2" gold strips for 72 Unit D. (**Diagram 6**)

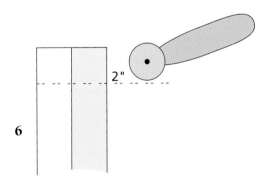

2"

6

7. Sew 2" brown and 2" ecru strips together. Repeat for three more strip sets. Cut at 2" intervals for 72 Unit E. (**Diagram 7**)

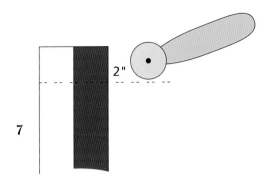

2"

7

8. For rows 1 and 5, sew A and B together. (**Diagram 8**)

8

A   B

9. For rows 2 and 4, sew a D and E to opposite ends of a 2" x 3 1/2" ecru rectangle. (**Diagram 9**)

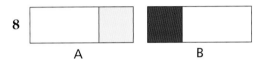

9

D   E

10. For row 3, sew a C to opposite sides of signed 3 1/2" x 6 1/2" rectangles noting position. (**Diagram 10**)

10

C   C

11. Sew rows together to complete block. (**Diagram 11**) Make a total of 36 blocks.

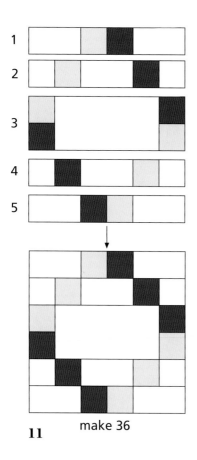

1
2
3
4
5

make 36

11

Finishing

1. Place blocks in six rows of six blocks in each row. Refer to quilt layout or use alternate layouts. (**Diagram 12**)

2. Sew blocks together in rows, then sew rows together.

3. Measure quilt lengthwise; piece and cut two 6½"-wide brown strips to that length. Sew to sides of quilt. Measure quilt crosswise; piece and cut two 6½"-wide brown strips to that length. Sew to top and bottom of quilt.

Optional: *Read Printing Photos to Fabric, pages 121 to 122, and print assorted photos onto prepared fabric sheets. Referring to Easy Appliqué, pages 119 to 120, appliqué randomly on border.*

4. Refer to Finishing Your Quilt, pages 123 to 127, to complete your quilt.

12

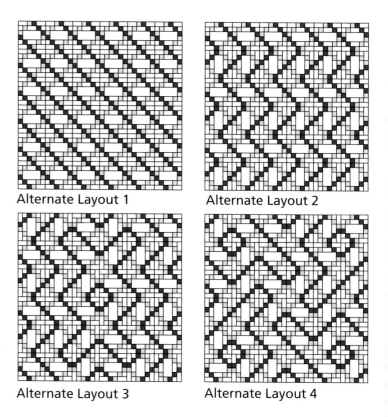

Alternate Layout 1   Alternate Layout 2

Alternate Layout 3   Alternate Layout 4

High School Memories Quilt Layout

"The quilt now not only keeps her warm as a cover for her bed, but also always reminds her of warm friendships and the friends she doesn't want to lose."

Wedding of the Stars

by Rita Weiss

Because my second daughter's marriage coincided with my entry into the fascinating world of quilt making, it seemed logical that I would make her a wedding quilt.

"We won't have a wedding book for the guests to sign," I declared. "Instead each guest will sign a square, and I'll put the squares into a quilt." At that time a company was selling small squares bordered with make-believe printed patchwork fabric which were intended for signatures.

At the wedding the guests happily signed the squares, and I began to plan the quilt. No matter what configuration I planned, the squares weren't working. For two years, I sketched and sketched. Finally I cut off the borders around each square. Now I had 32 plain signed squares with which to work.

Other projects seemed to take precedence, but I kept returning to the squares with the comment, "I'm going to finish this soon," as I put them back in the bottom of the "projects to be completed" box.

Deciding that I needed a picture of the bride and groom, I took classes wherever I could find them, on how to put photos on fabric. The discovery of the star fabric (my son-in-law loved the TV series, "Star Trek") moved the squares to the front row for a while.

Ten years passed, and another daughter was planning her wedding. I heard myself saying, "We'll have the guests sign a square…." My first son-in-law looked longingly at me and said very quietly, "Will we ever get our quilt?"

I never started the second wedding quilt. Before the next wedding, I finished the original wedding quilt.

It took a long time, but my son-in-law declared, "It was worth it."

You've got to love that guy.

—Rita Weiss

Wedding of the Stars

Approximate Size: 38" x 38"

Materials

photo that will finish $4^{1}/2$" x $6^{1}/2$"
*prepared fabric sheet (center photo)
$1/2$ yard muslin (signature squares)
$1/2$ yard gold lamé
$1/4$ yard light blue
$1/4$ yard medium blue
$1/4$ yard dark blue
$1/2$ yard very dark blue (includes binding)
1 yard backing
batting
$1/2$ yard fusible interfacing
freezer paper
1" plastic ring
   *Purchase prepared fabric sheet or refer to Preparing Your
Own Fabric for Printing, page 121, to make your own.

Cutting

Note: *Following manufacturer's instructions, fuse
interfacing to gold lamé before cutting. Use a press cloth to
press gold lamé.*

Signature Blocks

32 squares, $2^{3}/4$" x $2^{3}/4$", muslin
12 strips, $7/8$"-wide, gold lamé/interfacing
   cut into 64 strips, $7/8$" x $2^{3}/4$" and
   64 strips, $7/8$" x $3^{1}/2$"
24 squares, $3^{1}/4$" x $3^{1}/4$", light blue
   cut in half diagonally
24 squares, $3^{1}/4$" x $3^{1}/4$", medium blue
   cut in half diagonally
16 squares, $3^{1}/4$" x $3^{1}/4$", dark blue
   cut in half diagonally

Photo Block

Note: *Fuse 9" x 12" freezer paper to 9" x 12" muslin.*
$8^{1}/2$" x 11" rectangle, muslin/freezer paper
2 strips, $7/8$" x 7", gold lamé/interfacing
2 strips, $7/8$" x $5^{3}/4$", gold lamé/interfacing
1 square, 5" x 5":, very dark blue
   cut in half diagonally
1 square 6" x 6", very dark blue
   cut in half diagonally

Finishing

2 squares, $10^{1}/2$" x $10^{1}/2$", very dark blue (star points)
   cut in half diagonally
4 strips, $2^{1}/2$"-wide, very dark blue (binding)

Instructions

Signature Blocks

1. Sew $7/8$" x $2^{3}/4$" gold lamé strips to opposite sides of a
$2^{3}/4$" muslin square. Press seams toward gold lame.
(**Diagram 1**)

2. Sew $7/8$" x $3^{1}/2$" gold lamé strips to remaining sides of
the $2^{3}/4$" muslin square. Press seams toward gold lamé.
(**Diagram 2**)

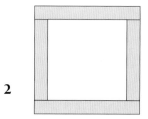

3. Sew light blue triangles to opposite sides of framed
square; press seams toward triangles. Sew light blue
triangles to remaining sides; press seams toward triangles.
(**Diagram 3**) **Note:** *Triangles are oversized to allow for
trimming.*

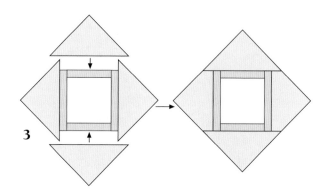

4. Trim resulting square to 5" x 5". (**Diagram 4**)

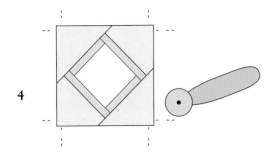

4

5. Repeat steps 1 to 4 for 11 more light blue Signature blocks. Repeat steps 1 to 4 for 12 medium blue Signature blocks and eight dark blue Signature blocks. (**Diagram 5**)

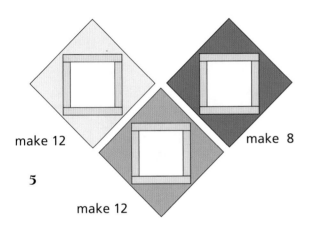

make 12

make 8

5

make 12

Photo Block

1. Referring to Printing Photos to Fabric, pages 121 to 122 and print photo to prepared fabric sheet. Trim photo to 5" x 7".

2. Sew $7/8$" x 7" gold lamé strips to opposite sides of photo; press toward gold lamé. Sew $7/8$" x $53/4$" gold lamé strips to remaining sides of photo; press toward gold lamé. (**Diagram 6**)

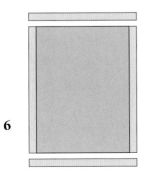

6

3. Sew 5" very dark blue triangles to top and bottom of photo; press seams toward triangles. Sew 6" triangles to sides of photo; press seams towards triangles. (**Diagram 7**)

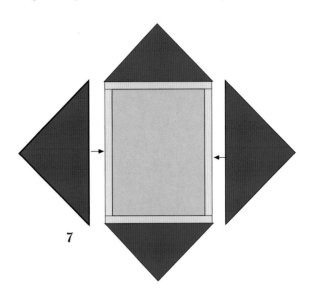

7

Finishing

1. Sew dark blue signature squares in pairs for a total of four pairs. Repeat with light blue and medium blue signature squares for four pairs of each. (**Diagram 8**)

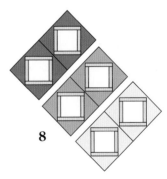

8

2. Sew a medium blue and light blue signature square together; repeat. Repeat two more times switching placement of the light blue and medium blue squares. (**Diagram 9**)

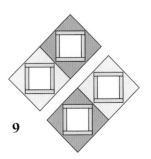

9

3. Sew pairs of squares to form the units in **Diagram 10.**

4. Sew photo block and signature units together. **Diagram 11**)

5. Center the 10½" very dark blue triangles on each side of quilt top; sew and press in place. (**Diagram 12**)

6. Layer quilt top with batting and backing. **Note:** *Do not cut batting and backing at this time. Quilt as desired.*

7. Trim batting and backing even with quilt top edges.

8. Sew binding to quilt, working inner corners and mitering outer corners as shown in Attaching the Continuous Machine Binding, pages 125 to 126.

9. Add rod pocket to back of quilt referring to Adding a Rod Pocket, pages 126 to 127. Attach a 1" plastic ring at tip of top point. (**Diagram 13**)

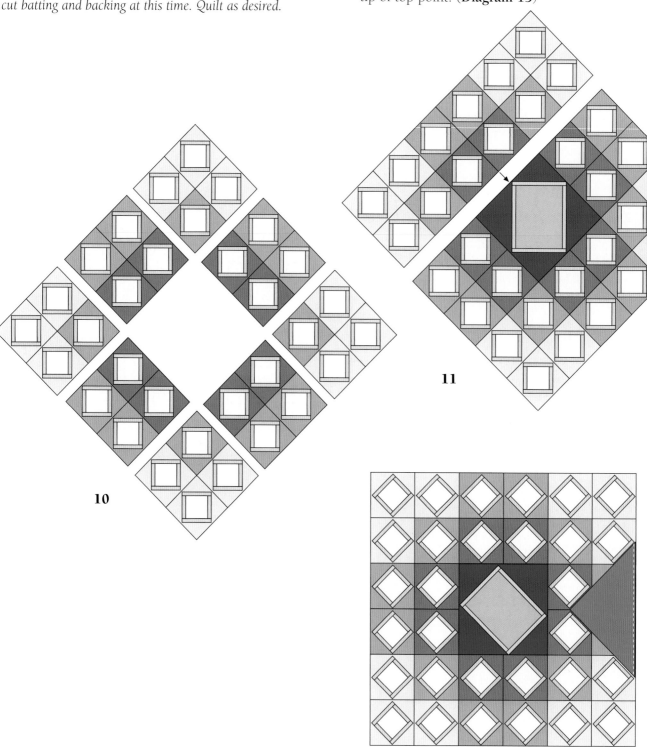

10

11

12

Wedding of the Stars
Quilt Layout

"It took a long time,
but my son-in-law
declared, 'It was
worth it.' You've got to
love that guy."

13

Crazy for Baseball

by Linda Causee

Always a fan of baseball, I am especially fond of my home team, the San Diego Padres.

Often when you attend a home game, you are presented with a Padres pin, and I have collected many pins over the years. To protect my skin from the bright sun at games, I always wore a hat to which I would attach my pins. Eventually the collection became so large that the pins began to weigh down the hat so much that I often experienced headaches after each ballgame.

No longer able to wear my entire collection to games, I kept trying to come up with a way to showcase it. I just didn't want to bury my pins in a drawer. Imagine my delight when I discovered fabric printed with the Padres logo! As soon as I saw the fabric, I knew how I could use it. I'd make a quilt to showcase my pin collection.

I quickly created the baseball diamond for the center and using the foundation piecing method, I made the crazy quilt blocks for the sides.

Now there's room for more and more Padre pins.

Go, Padres!....or whatever team you are rooting for.

—*Linda Causee*

Crazy for Baseball

Approximate Size: 42" x 42"

Materials

3/4 yard baseball novelty print

fat quarters of assorted coordinating and
    contrasting fabrics

fat quarter white print

1 yard green (includes second border)

1/4 yard light brown

1/4 yard dark brown

1 1/4 yards backing

1/2 yard blue print (binding)

craft-size thin batting

Patterns (pages 59 and 60)

Foundation Square

Foundation Triangle

Cutting

Blocks

Note: *You do not need to cut exact pieces for foundation piecing the blocks.*

Finishing

1 square, 15" x 15", green (center)

4 strips, 3 1/4" x 15", light brown (inside border)

4 squares, 3 1/4" x 3 1/4", white print (inside cornerstones)

4 strips, 1 1/2"-wide, dark brown (first border)

4 strips, 2 1/2"-wide, green (second border)

5 strips, 4 1/2"-wide, novelty print (third border)

5 strips, 2 1/2"-wide, blue (binding)

Instructions

1. Make four square foundations and eight triangle foundations referring to Preparing the Foundation, page 114. (**Diagram 1**)

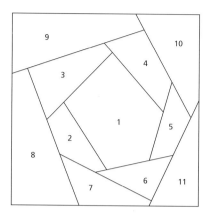

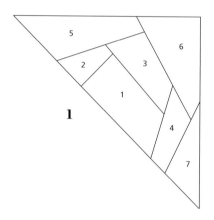

2. Piece foundation blocks referring to Making a Foundation Pieced Block, pages 115 to 119. (**Diagram 2**)

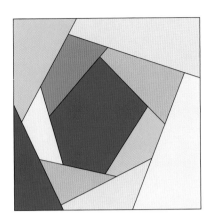

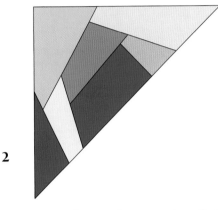

2

3. Sew pieced triangles to adjacent sides of pieced squares. (**Diagram 3**)

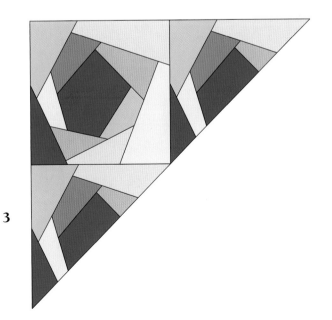

3

4. Sew 3¹/4" x 15" light brown strips to opposite sides of 15" green square. Sew a 3¹/4" x 3¹/4" white print square to opposite sides of remaining two 3¹/4" x 15" light brown strips, then sew to top and bottom of green square. (**Diagram 4**)

4

5. Sew pieced triangles to opposite sides of quilt center; sew pieced triangles to remaining sides. (**Diagram 5**)

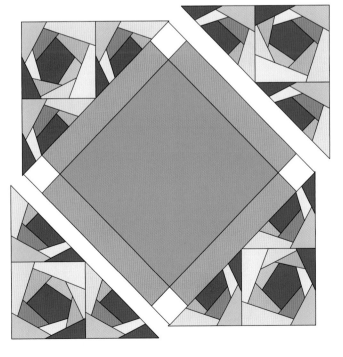

5

6. Measure quilt lengthwise; cut two 1¹/2" dark brown strips to that length. Sew to sides of quilt. Measure quilt crosswise; cut two 1¹/2" dark brown strips to that length. Sew to top and bottom of quilt.

7. Repeat step 6 for remaining two borders.

8. Refer to Finishing Your Quilt, pages 123 to 127, to complete the quilt.

9. Add pins and memorabilia as desired in center green portion of quilt.

"No longer able to wear my entire collection to games, I kept trying to come up with a way to showcase it. I just didn't want to bury my pins in a drawer."

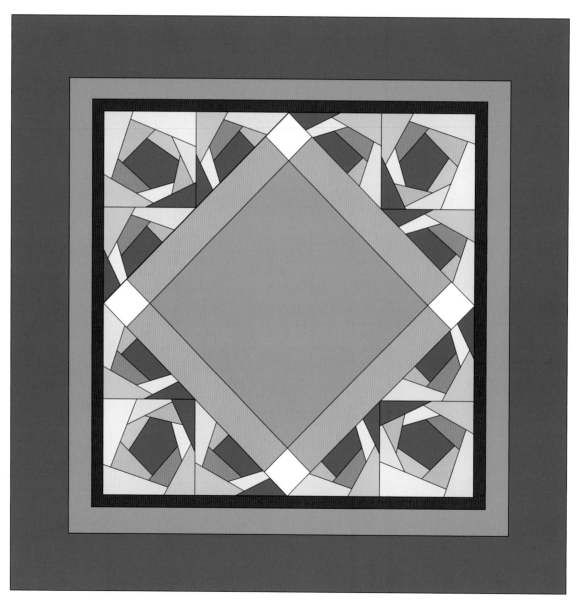

Crazy For Baseball Quilt Layout

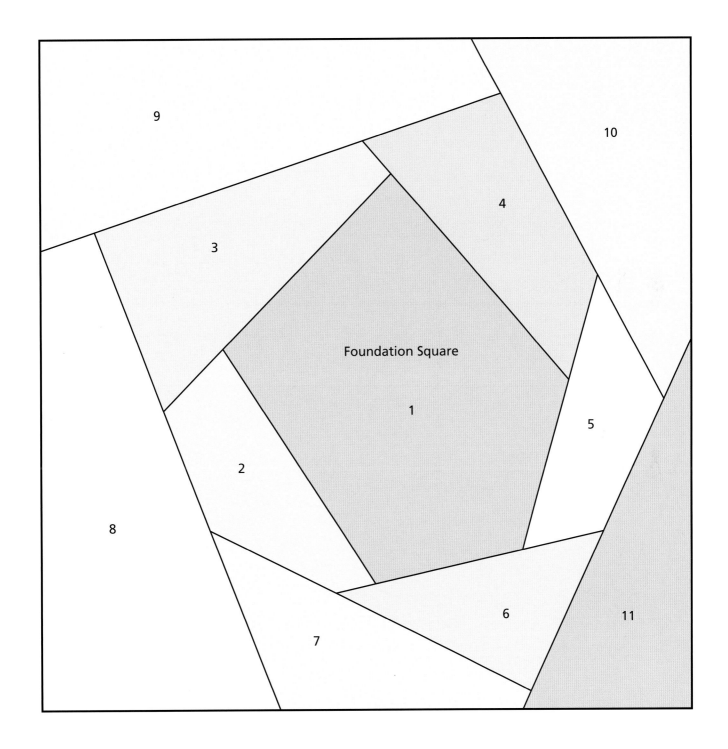

9

10

3

4

Foundation Square

1

5

2

8

6

11

7

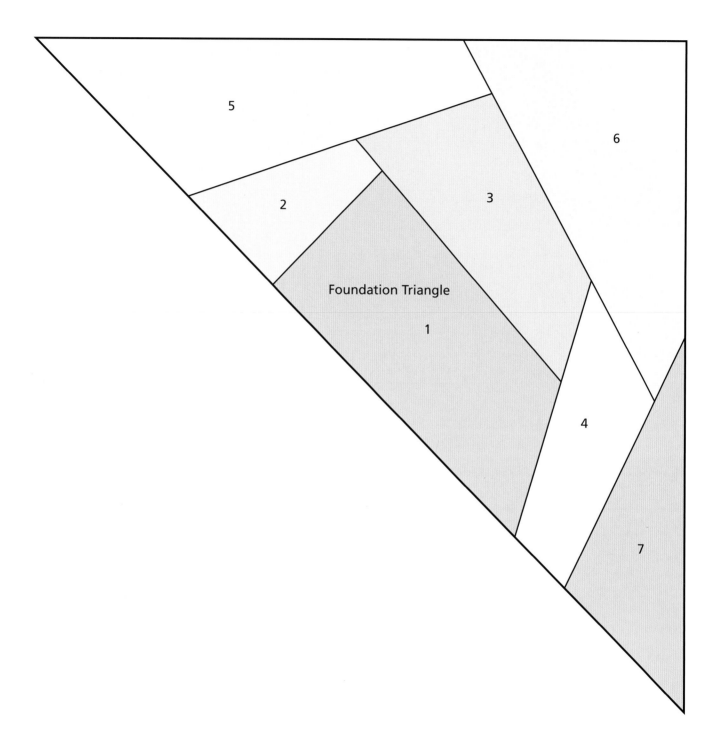

Crazy For Baseball Pattern Piece

5

6

2

3

Foundation Triangle

1

4

7

"I quickly created the baseball diamond for the center and using the foundation piecing method, I made the crazy quilt blocks for the sides ...now there's room for more and more Padre pins."

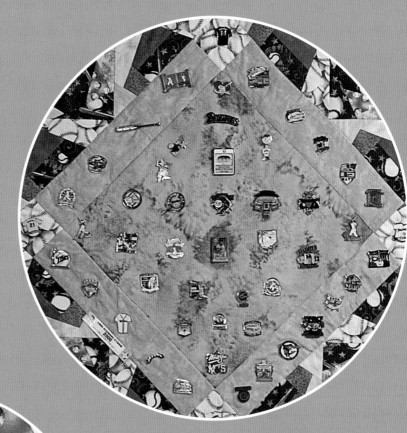

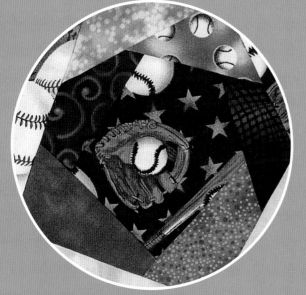

My Pin Collection

by Rita Weiss

When Linda showed me her "Crazy for Baseball" quilt on page 54, my first comment was, "I collect pins too." They may not be baseball pins, but they represent something that I'm crazy about as well. My pins come from quilt shows that I have attended over the past twenty-five years.

I took Linda's plan for her quilt, decreased the measurements so that instead of 42" x 42", my quilt is 21" x 21" and uses fabric printed with sewing motifs rather than baseball. It's actually the same quilt only smaller, allowing plenty of room for additional pins.

Go quilters!....or for whatever hobby you are collecting pins.

—Rita Weiss

My Pin Collection

Approximate Size: 21" x 21"

Materials

1/4 yard yard quilting print 1
 (block centers and inside border)
scraps of assorted coordinating and
 contrasting fabrics
fat quarter light blue (center square)
1/4 yard black (first border)
1/2 yard red
 (second border, binding)
3/8 yard quilting print 2 (third border)
1/2 yard backing
thin batting

Patterns (page 66)

Foundations Square
Foundation Triangle

Cutting

Blocks

Note: *You do not need to cut exact pieces for foundation piecing the blocks.*

Finishing

1 square, 7 1/2" x 7 1/2", light blue
 (center)
2 strips, 2" x 7 1/2", quilting print 1
 (inside border)
2 strips, 2" x 10 1/2", quilting print 1
 (inside border)
4 strips, 1"-wide, black (first border)
4 strips, 1 1/2"-wide, red
 (second border)
4 strips, 2 1/2"-wide, quilting print 2
 (third border)
4 strips, 2 1/2"-wide, red (binding)

Instructions

1. Make four square foundations and eight triangle foundations referring to Preparing the Foundation, page 114. (**Diagram 1**)

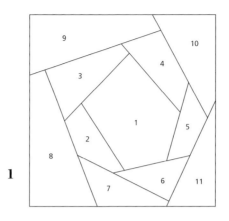 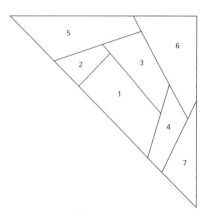

1

2. Piece foundation blocks referring to Making the Block, pages 115 to 119. (**Diagram 2**)

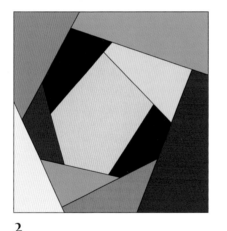 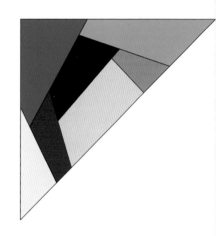

2

3. Sew pieced triangles to adjacent sides of pieced squares. (**Diagram 3**)

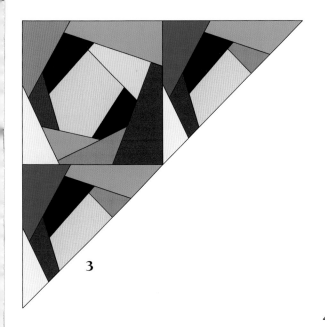

3

4

4. Sew 2" x 7$\frac{1}{2}$" quilting print 1 strips to opposite sides of 7$\frac{1}{2}$" light blue square; sew 2" x 10$\frac{1}{2}$" quilting print 1 strips to remaining sides for quilt center. (**Diagram 4**)

5. Sew pieced triangles to opposite sides of quilt center; sew pieced triangles to remaining sides. (**Diagram 5**)

5

6. Measure quilt lengthwise; cut two 1" black strips to that length. Sew to sides of quilt. Measure quilt crosswise; cut two 1" black strips to that length. Sew to top and bottom of quilt.

7. Repeat step 6 for remaining two borders.

8. Refer to Finishing Your Quilt, pages 123 to 127, to complete the quilt.

9. Add pins and memorabilia as desired in center light blue portion of quilt.

My Pin Collection Pattern Pieces

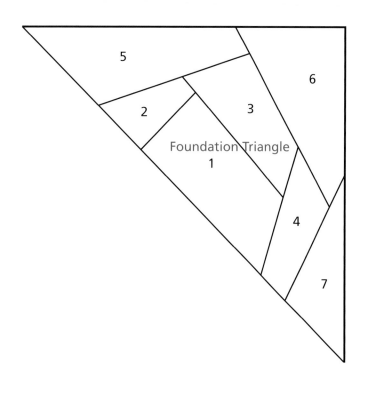

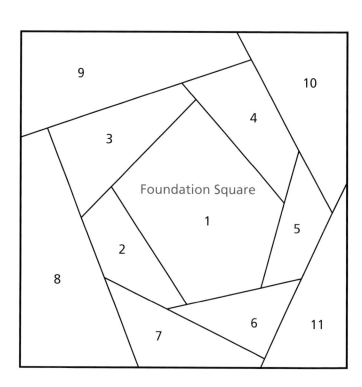

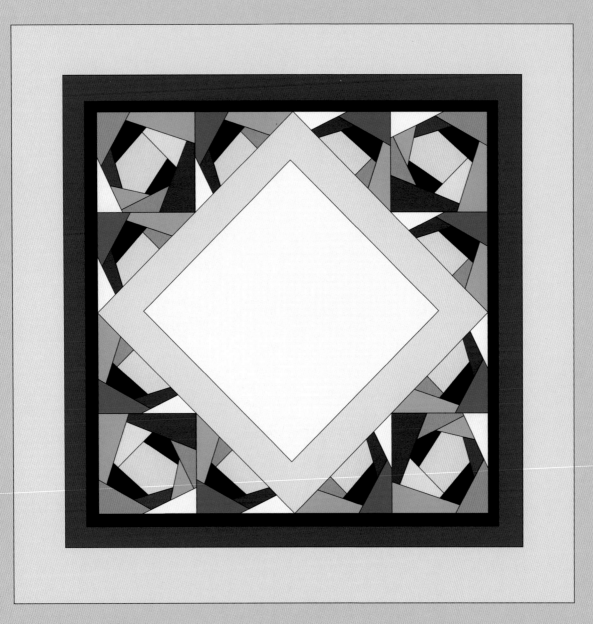

My Pin Collection Quilt Layout

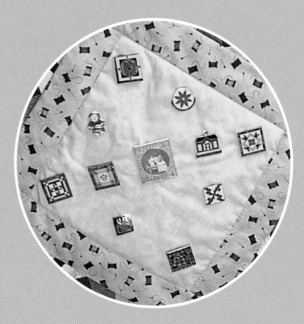

"Go quilters!....

or for whatever

hobby you are

collecting pins...."

Grandma's Hankies

by Linda Causee

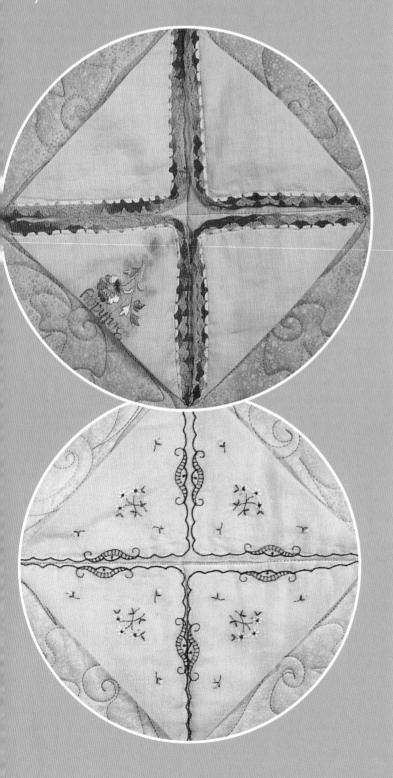

My grandmother was a remarkable lady. She loved her flower garden and she loved to crochet. Despite raising a large family and caring for a household when labor-saving gadgets were not available, she still found time for her loves. She spent hours crocheting edgings on handkerchiefs and cultivating roses.

My grandmother would never think of using a paper tissue. Not her and certainly not her children. One wasn't completely dressed without a freshly laundered and beautifully ironed linen handkerchief in your pocket.

When my grandmother died, there were many, many handkerchiefs in her drawers. We had now entered the days of paper tissues, and no one wanted the handkerchiefs. I asked for and received my grandmother's handkerchiefs. I wasn't certain what I would do with them, but I knew that I didn't want them destroyed.

For many years, grandma's hankies sat in a box in my dresser drawer. I'd take them out occasionally, look at them, and think of my grandmother. Then I'd put them away and forget about the handkerchiefs and, sadly to say, my grandmother.

When I began the quilting hobby, it occurred to me that I could put grandma's handker-chiefs into a quilt which I would see everyday and thereby be reminded of her.

It took me a long time to decide how to design the quilt because I couldn't bear the thought of cutting up the hankies. Finally I hit upon the idea of folding them and sewing each hankie on to a background square, thereby preserving the hankies but still using them in the quilt.

And, the floral sashing fabric: that's grand-mother's flower garden.

—Linda Causee

Grandma's Hankies

Approximate Size: 72" x 86"

Materials

30 Hankies

3/4 yard each light pink, light yellow, light green,
  light blue, light purple (background)

1/2 yard each six different pastel floral prints (sashing)

1/4 yard floral print (cornerstones)

5/8 yard binding

7 yards backing

full-size batting

Cutting

Blocks

6 squares each, 12$\frac{1}{2}$" x 12$\frac{1}{2}$", light pink, light yellow,
  light green, light blue, light purple

Finishing

5 strips each, 2$\frac{1}{2}$"-wide, pastel floral prints (sashing)

42 squares, 2$\frac{1}{2}$" x 2$\frac{1}{2}$", pastel floral print (cornerstones)

8 strips, 2$\frac{1}{2}$"-wide, ivory (binding)

Instructions

1. Fold corners of hankies toward center, wrong sides together. (**Diagram 1**) Press.

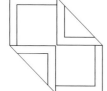

1

2. Center folded hanky on a background square. (**Diagram 2**)

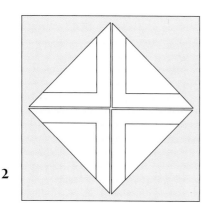

2

3. Using invisible thread, sew hanky along lacy edges of hankies. (**Diagram 3**)

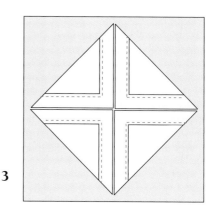

3

Hint: *There are several options for finishing the folded edges of the hankies:*

　　(1) You can keep them loose

　　(2) Sew down with a small machine zigzag and
　　　　invisible thread

　　(3) Sew down using a decorative machine stitch and
　　　　matching or contrasting thread

　　(4) hand embroider using your favorite stitch

4. Repeat steps 2 and 3 for remaining hankies and backgrounds.

Finishing

1. Sew 2$\frac{1}{2}$"-wide pastel floral print strips together in sets of six. (**Diagram 4**)

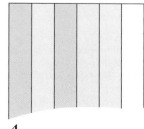

4

2. Cut strip sets at 2$\frac{1}{2}$" intervals to make sashing strips. (**Diagram 5**) You will need a total of 71 sashing strips.

3. Arrange blocks, sashing and cornerstones referring to Quilt Layout.

4. Sew blocks and sashing rows. Sew sashing and cornerstone rows. (**Diagram 6**)

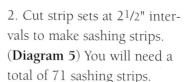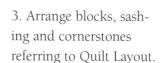

2$\frac{1}{2}$"

2$\frac{1}{2}$"

5

5. Sew rows together.

6. Refer to Finishing Your Quilt, pages 123 to 127, to complete your quilt.

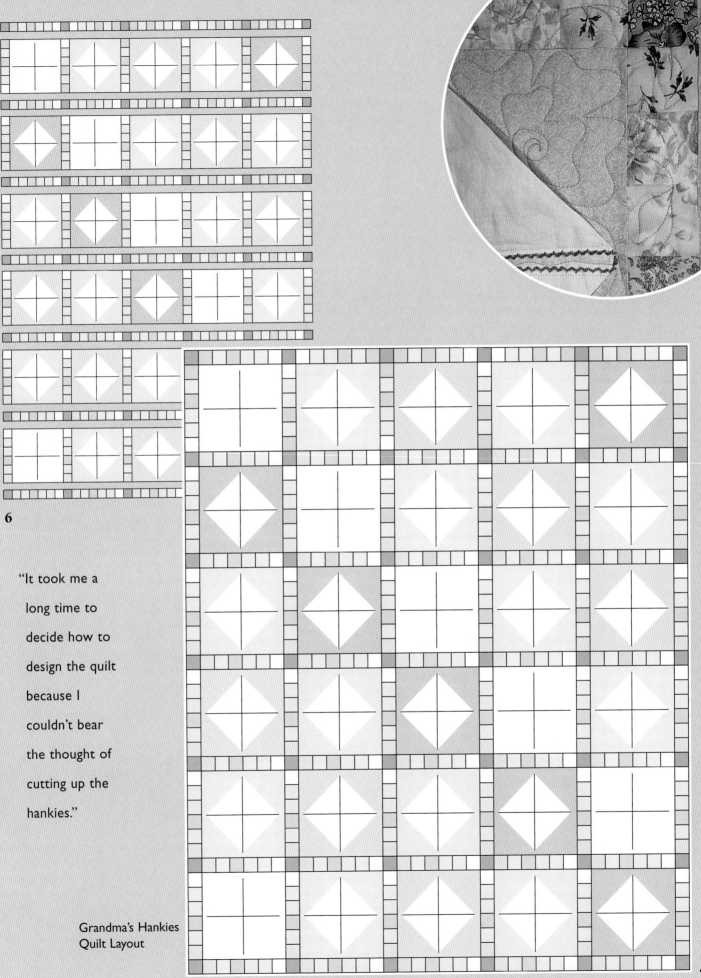

"It took me a
long time to
decide how to
design the quilt
because I
couldn't bear
the thought of
cutting up the
hankies."

Grandma's Hankies
Quilt Layout

Love Letters

by Rita Weiss

My husband and I have always encouraged our daughters to express themselves through the written word. They were, therefore, constantly sending us messages and notes.

For a long time we had a bulletin board in our kitchen, and the notes, messages, poems, letters would be posted on the bulletin board. I loved re-reading the messages as the notes often hung for several years.

I called the bulleting board "My Love Letters" because I loved receiving them, and I hoped that the sender loved sending them.

When we moved from the house with the bulletin board, I kept my love letters in a file drawer under "L". I hoped to one day restore my bulletin board and my love letters. After several years, however, the paper upon which the love letters had been written began to disintegrate, and the new house didn't have the room for a bulletin board.

It was a simple transition to change the original bulletin board into a quilt, preserving the love letters on fabric, and to hang them on the quilt, securing with buttons instead of tacks. Fabric envelopes replaced the paper ones, and several of the love letters can actually be removed from their envelopes and read, just as they were in the original bulletin board.

Choosing which Love Letters to hang on my quilt was a big chore. I have more in the file, and I'm planning my second Love Letter quilt right now.

If you have some Love Letters, why not make your own bulletin board, but be careful which love letters you pick for your quilt. The letters will be there for everyone to read.

—*Rita Weiss*

Love Letters

Approximate Size: 40" x 28"

Materials

3/4 yard dark green
5/8 yard wood grain print (includes binding)
fat quarters white, light colors
7/8 yard backing
craft-size thin batting
*prepared fabric sheets
1/2 - 1 yard heavyweight interfacing
1 yard paper-backed fusible web
assorted cards and notes
assorted buttons
invisible nylon thread

Use purchased fabric sheets or refer to Preparing Your Own Fabric for Printing, page 121, to make your own.

Cutting

1 rectangle, 24$^{1}/2$" x 36$^{1}/2$", dark green
2 strips, 2$^{1}/2$" x 24$^{1}/2$", wood grain print (side border)
2 strips, 2$^{1}/2$" x 40$^{1}/2$", wood grain print
    (top and bottom border)
4 strips, 2$^{1}/2$"-side, woodgrain print (binding)

Instructions

1. For bulletin board quilt, sew the 2$^{1}/2$" x 24$^{1}/2$" wood grain print strips to short sides of dark green rectangle. Press seams toward border. Sew the 2$^{1}/2$" x 40$^{1}/2$" wood grain print strips to top and bottom. Press seams toward border. (**Diagram 1**)

1

2. Refer to Finishing Your Quilt, pages 123 to 127, to complete quilt.

3. Referring to Printing Photos to Fabric, pages 121 to 122, print cards and notes onto prepared fabric sheets. Be sure to print both front and back of cards. Rough cut printed cards and notes.

4. Iron paper-backed fusible web to the wrong side of printed notes and front side only of printed cards. Remove paper backing and fuse to heavywieght interfacing. Cut out fused notes and card fronts. (**Diagram 2**)

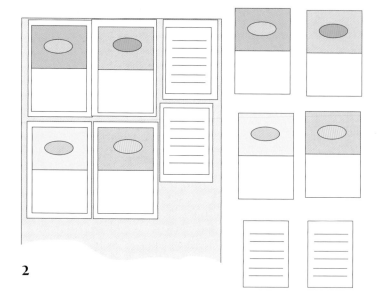

2

5. Cut out the back side of cards and fuse to backs (interfacing side) of corresponding fronts. Trim card so front and back edges are even. **Optional:** *Finish edges with machine zigzag and invisible thread.* Set aside.

6. Notes that are not two-sided will need to be backed with plain fabric to cover the interfacing. Iron paper-backed fusible web to wrong side of enough white fabric to cover backs of notes. Remove paper, then position notes right side up on fusible side of backing fabric. Cut out notes. Set aside. **Optional:** *Finish edges with machine zigzag and invisible thread.*

7. To make an envelope, cut two pieces of fabric, 6$^{1}/2$" x 12$^{1}/2$". Place fabric pieces right sides together on cutting mat. Mark midpoint of top side; mark 4$^{1}/4$" down from top along both sides. (**Diagram 3**)

8. Cut diagonally from top midpoint to marked points on each side. (**Diagram 4**)

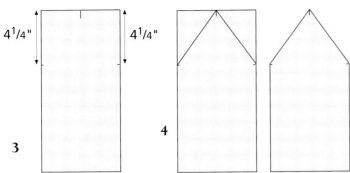

3

4¼"   4¼"

4

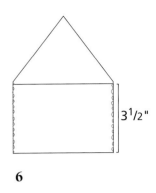

6

3½"

Note: *To make an envelope to fit your own cards, measure length and width of card. Cut the envelope fabric the length of the fabric plus ¹/2" by three times the width of the card plus ¹/2". So for a 5" x 7" card, cut fabric, 15¹/2" x 7¹/2".*

9. Keeping fabric pieces right sides together, sew along all edges using ¹/4" seam allowance leaving a 3" - 4" opening along lower edge. (**Diagram 5**)

10. Turn envelope right side out through opening. Sew opening closed and press envelope. Fold bottom of envelope up about 3¹/2". Using invisible thread and a small machine zigzag, sew along both sides. (**Diagram 6**)

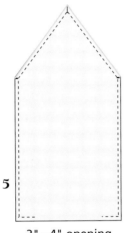

5

3" - 4" opening

11. Arrange notes and cards in desired arrangement on "bulletin board." Pin in place. Starting with one card at a time, position button on top corner and sew to card and bulletin board through all layers.

12. Attach envelope to bulletin board using a button, then place a card or note inside envelope so it peeks out through opening. Repeat for all envelopes and cards.

"...be careful which love letters you pick for your quilt. The letters will be there for everyone to read."

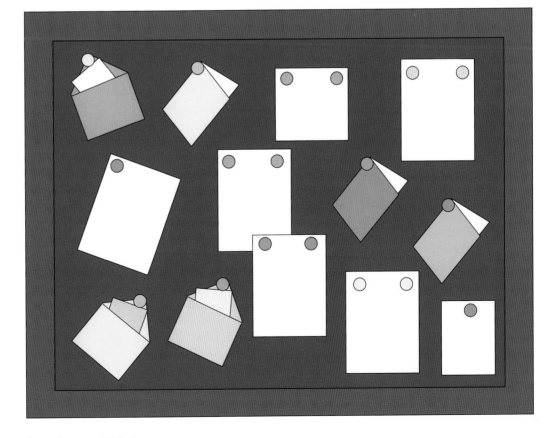

Love Letters Quilt Layout

75

Sunbonnet Sue is Wearing My Clothes

by Linda Causee

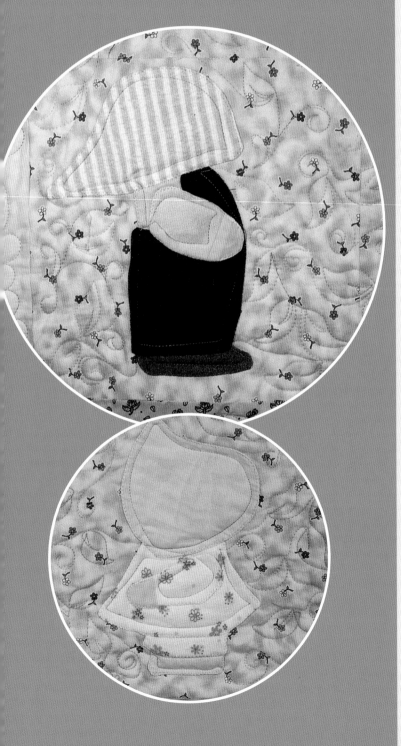

I made this quilt for a dear friend of mine who became a grandmother for the first time. After raising three sons, her first grandchild was a girl, and grandma doted upon this little bundle.

Nothing was beyond reach for grandma who supplied the new darling with little dresses and hats.

Unfortunately babies grow fast and soon the darling had outgrown most of her adorable outfits. The new grandmother told me how sad she was to find a stack of clothes in the corner of the baby's bedroom that the little one had outgrown. The baby's parents did not want to dispose of the clothes their baby had worn, but they simply didn't have room.

Why not do what our grandmothers had always done: use pieces of outworn clothes in a quilt? And, what better way to use them in a quilt than to have Sunbonnet Sue and her pal Overall Sam wear clothes made from the clothes that this little granddaughter had worn? The baby garments were cut up and used to make the clothes worn by Sue and Sam and were pieced to create the pieced border of the quilt. Other co-ordinating fabrics make up the paths that Sue and Sam follow as well as their toys and their puppy.

The little granddaughter will grow up and wear other outfits, but Sunbonnet Sue and Overall Sam will always wear her baby clothes!

—Linda Causee

Sunbonnet Sue is Wearing My Clothes

Approximate Size: 68" x 59"

Materials
Assorted baby clothes
  (Sue and Sam clothing and pieced border)
Assorted scraps (extras)
1¹/2 yards light blue (background)
1¹/2 yards green floral print 1 (background)
1¹/4 yards green floral print 2 (background, third border)
³/8 yard beige (background)
¹/2 yard light pink (first border)
¹/2 yard medium pink (binding)
3¹/2 yards backing
twin-size batting
2 yards fusible interfacing
2 yards lightweight paper-backed fusible web
template plastic
permanent black marker
permanent fabric markers (black, green)
invisible nylon thread

Patterns (pages 82-86)
Sunbonnet Sue A
Sunbonnet Sue B
Overall Sam
Kite, Bird, Butterfly
Flower, Wagon, Puppy, Ladybug

Cutting
Blocks
10 squares, 9¹/2" x 9¹/2", light blue (A, C)
1 rectangle, 4¹/2" x 9¹/2", light blue (B)
1 square, 9⁷/8" x 9⁷/8", light blue (D)
  Cut in half diagonally.
12 squares, 9¹/2" x 9¹/2", green floral print 1 (E)
1 rectangle, 4¹/2" x 9¹/2", green floral print 1 (B)
1 square, 4¹/2" x 4¹/2", green floral print 1 (C)
3 squares, 9⁷/8" x 9⁷/8", green floral print 2 (D, G)
  Cut in half diagonally.
2 squares, 9¹/2" x 9¹/2", beige (F)
2 squares, 9⁷/8" x 9⁷/8", beige (G)

Finishing
6 strips, 2¹/2"-wide, pink (first border)
100 squares, 2¹/2" x 2¹/2", assorted baby clothes
  (second border)
6 strips, 3¹/2"-wide, green floral print 2 (third border)
6 strips, 2¹/2"-wide, medium pink (binding)

Instructions

1. Trace patterns for Sunbonnet Sue A, Sunbonnet Sue B and Overall Sam onto template plastic using a black permanent marker. (**Diagram 1**) Cut out patterns.

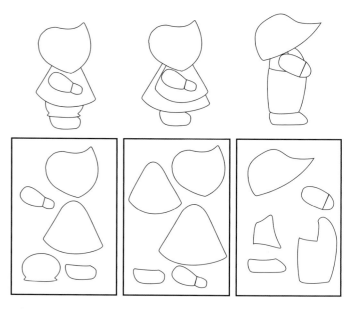

1

2. Trace patterns onto wrong side of chosen baby clothes. Use the templates as drawn for Sue and Sam facing right. Flop the patterns if you would like Sue and Sam to face left. Note that three Sunbonnet Sue A are facing right and one is facing left; one Sunbonnet Sue B is facing right and one left; and two Overall Sam figures are facing left and two are facing right. Also, to change the look of Sue, add the apron to Sunbonnet Sue A and eliminate it from Sunbonnet Sue B. Sam can also wear his hat backwards by flopping pattern when tracing.

3. After tracing patterns, cut out about ¹/4" from drawn line.

Hint: *For arm/hand piece, sew a 2" x 3" baby fabric rectangle to a 2" x 2" peach (hand) fabric. Trace and cut out the hand and arm as one template and place on wrong side of rectangle and square just sewn, lining up seam with line separating hand from arm. Trace around template, then cut out 1/4" from drawn line.* (**Diagram 2**)

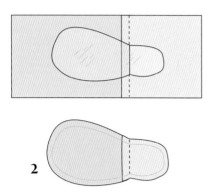

2

4. Rough cut interfacing pieces for each Sue and Sam piece. Place appliqué piece right side down on bumpy side of interfacing. Sew along drawn line. (**Diagram 3**) Trim interfacing even with fabric.

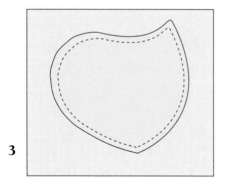

3

5. Cut a slit in center of interfacing and turn appliqué right side out. (**Diagram 4**)

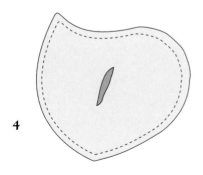

4

6. Repeat steps 2 to 5 for all appliqué pieces.

Hint: *If your baby clothes have a nice hemmed edge, you can place the lower edge of the dress or overalls patterns along the hemmed edge of fabric even if the hemmed edge does not curve with the pattern.* (**Diagram 5**)

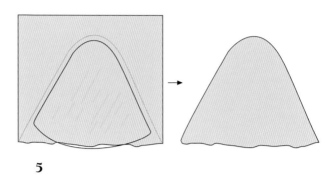

5

7. Make pieced background blocks as follows (**Diagram 6**):

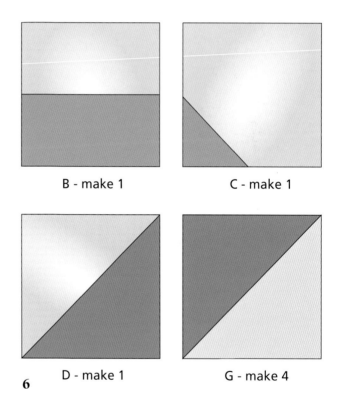

B - make 1

C - make 1

D - make 1

G - make 4

6

8. Position the Sunbonnet Sue and Overall Sam pieces onto background squares, noting positions. (**Diagram 7**) Iron pieces to fuse to background. Machine zigzag around pieces using invisible nylon thread.

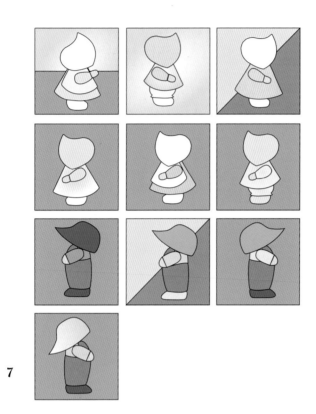

7

9. Trace patterns for two puppies, seven flowers, eight leaves, two birds, two butterflies, two ladybugs, one kite and one wagon onto paper side of paper-backed fusible web. Rough cut patterns and fuse to wrong side of desired fabrics according to manufacturer's directions. Cut out patterns along drawn lines.

10. Position remaining appliqué pieces from step 9 onto background squares. (**Diagram 8**) Fuse in place following manufacturer's directions.

11. Machine zigzag along raw edges of appliqués using invisible nylon thread.

12. Arrange blocks referring to quilt layout. Sew blocks together in rows, then sew rows together.

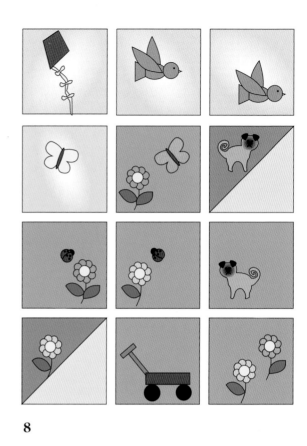

8

13. Using a green permanent fabric marker, draw stems for flowers. Using a black permanent fabric marker, draw kite string, ladybug dots, butterfly antennae, puppy faces, and birds' eyes and beaks.

14. Measure quilt top lengthwise. Piece and cut two 21/2"-wide pink strips to that length. Sew to sides of quilt. Measure quilt top crosswise. Piece and cut two 21/2"-wide pink strips to that length. Sew to top and bottom of quilt top.

15. Sew 22 assorted 21/2" squares together in random order. Repeat. Sew to sides of quilt. Sew 28 assorted 21/2" squares together and sew to top and bottom of quilt.

16. Measure quilt top lengthwise. Piece and cut two 31/2"-wide green floral print 2 strips to that length. Sew to sides of quilt. Measure quilt top crosswise. Piece and cut two 31/2"-wide floral green 2 print strips to that length. Sew to top and bottom of quilt.

17. Refer to Finishing Your Quilt, pages 123 to 127, to complete your quilt.

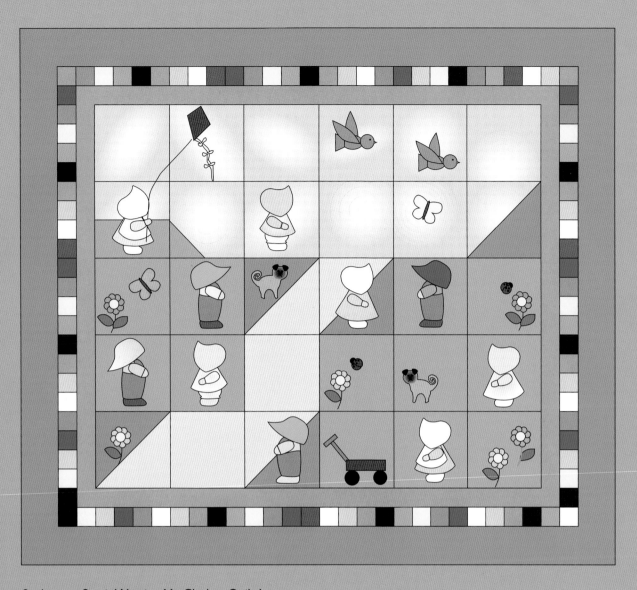

Sunbonnet Sue is Wearing My Clothes Quilt Layout

"Why not do what our grandmothers had always done: use pieces of out-worn clothes in a quilt?"

Sunbonnet Sue is Wearing My Clothes Pattern Pieces

Bird

Ladybug

Puppy

Butterfly

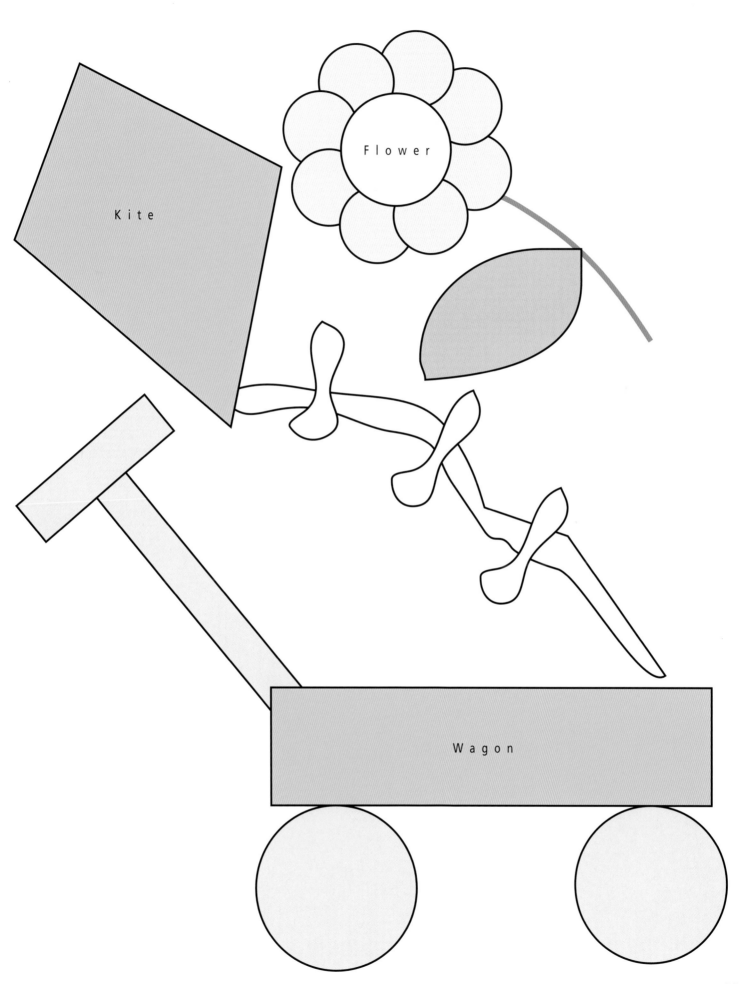

Kite

Flower

Wagon

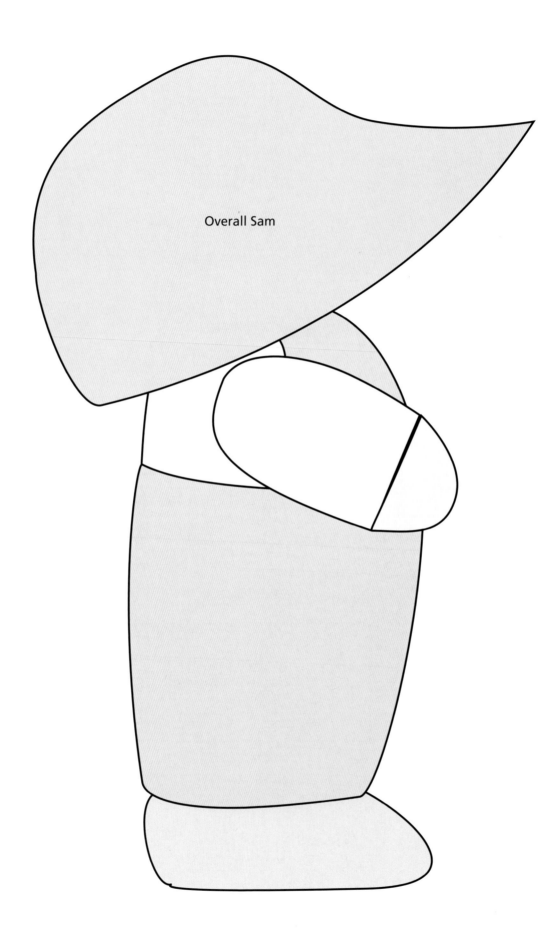

Overall Sam

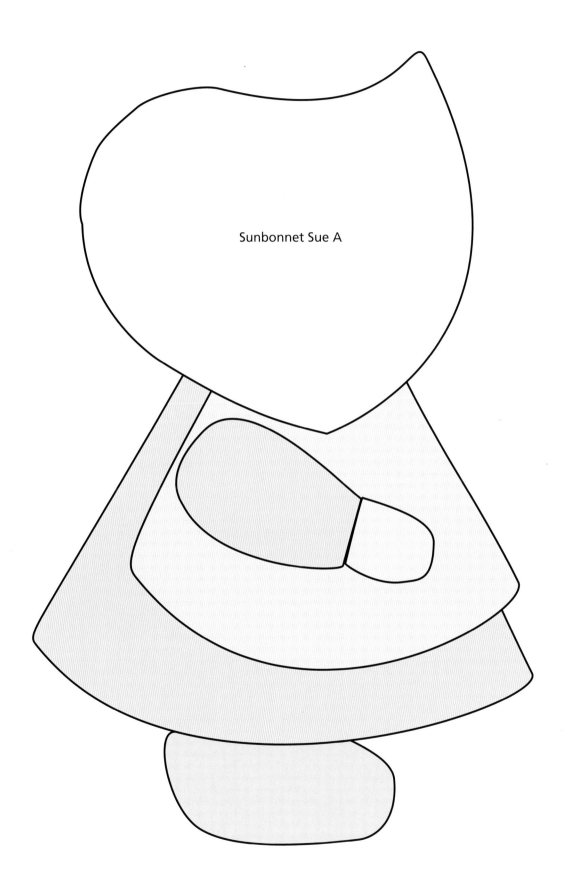

Sunbonnet Sue A

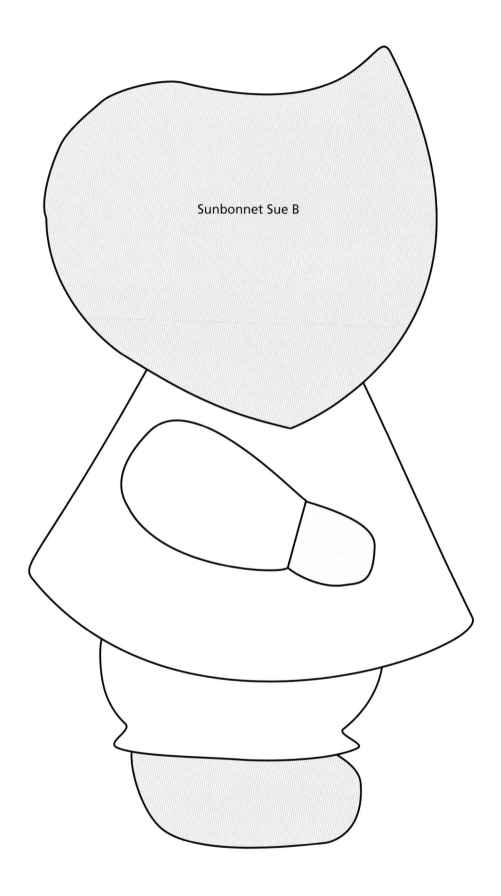

Sunbonnet Sue B

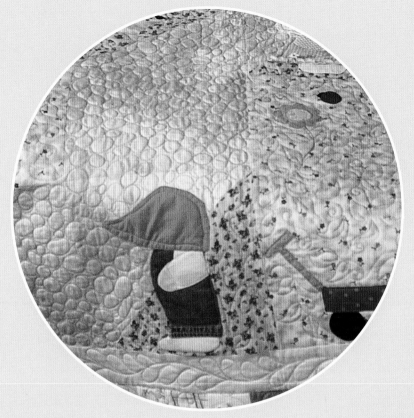

"The little
granddaughter
will grow
up and wear
other outfits, but
Sunbonnet Sue and
Overall Sam will
always wear her
baby clothes!"

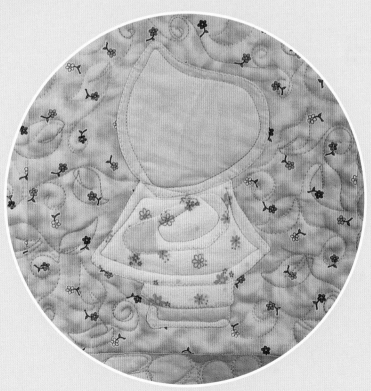

Musical Memories

by Rita Weiss

Have you ever attended an event at which the poster was almost more exciting than the event itself and so you kept the poster? Or, the event was one you wanted to keep in your memory?

I kept this poster for a long time because I liked the design and because I wanted to remember my daughter's senior college piano recital. The paper upon which the poster was printed was beginning to disintegrate, and I was afraid I'd finally have to throw the poster away.

The discovery of fabric that represented piano keys was the impetus toward putting my poster into a quilt. The reproduced poster now sits surrounded by music reviving old memories.

What is even more surprising is that I think I can actually hear the Schuman themes once again whenever I cast a glance at my poster quilt.

—*Rita Weiss*

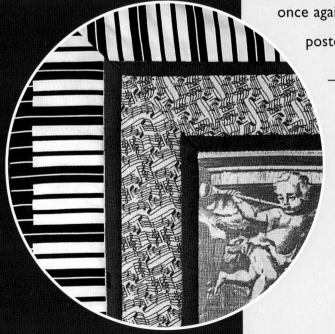

Musical Memories

Approximate Size: 14" x 17"

Materials

poster, announcement or other memorabilia
*prepared fabric sheet
1/2 yard red (includes binding)
1/4 yard red print
1/4 yard black print
15" x 18" rectangle thin batting
1/2 yard backing

*Purchase prepared fabric sheets or make your own referring to Preparing Your Own Fabric for Printing, page 121.

Cutting

4 strips, 3/4"-wide, red (first and third borders)
2 strips, 1 1/2"-wide, red print (second border)
2 strips, 2 1/4"-wide, black print (fourth borders)
3 strips, 2 1/2"-wide, red (binding)

Instructions

1. Referring to Printing Photos to Fabric, pages 121 to 122, print poster onto prepared fabric sheet. Trim 1/4" from outside edge of printed area of poster.

2. For borders, sew a 3/4" red strip, 1 1/2" red print strip, another 3/4" red strip and a 2 1/4" black print strip together. (**Diagram 1**) Repeat.

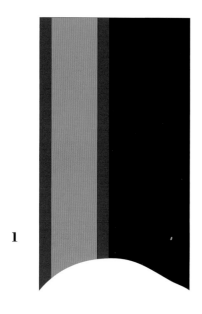

1

Note: *The width of the strips sets should be 3 3/4" and will finish 3 1/4". Measure the poster panel and the width of the strips sewn in step 2. The photographed quilt has a center that measures 7 1/2" x 10 1/2" (7" x 10" finished) and strip sets that measure 3 3/4" (3 1/4" finished).*

3. Measure the poster panel. The printed photographed quilt has a center that measures 7 1/2" x 10 1/2". (7" x 10" finished.)

4. The formula for cutting strip sets for mitered corners is:

finished width and length of quilt center plus twice the finished width of the strip sets plus 1/2" (7" + 3 1/4" + 3 1/4" + 1/2" = 14" and 10" + 3 1/4" + 3 1/4" + 1/2" = 17").

Cut strip sets as follows (**Diagram 2**):

2 strips, 14" long
2 strips, 17" long

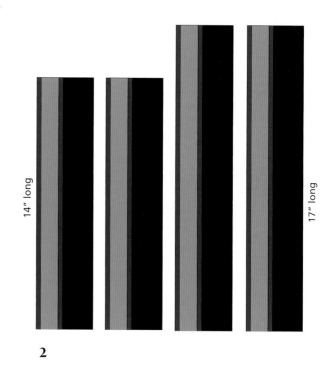

14" long   17" long

2

5. Refer to Mitered Borders, pages 122 to 123, to sew borders to center.

6. Refer to Finishing Your Quilt, pages 123 to 127, to complete your quilt.

Musical Memories Quilt Layout

"What is even more surprising is that I think I can actually hear the Schuman themes once again when I cast a glance at my poster quilt."

My Puppy's Pictures

by Linda Causee

When children grow up and leave home, there's always an emptiness in the household. That's when I decided to get a puppy. We had owned dogs before, but they belonged to the children. This puppy, Angel the Pug, was my new baby.

Don't tell my children, but in many ways a puppy is better than a child. She learned to listen very quickly, and she never asked to borrow the car. She doesn't bring home strange friends, or ask for money. She loves only me; she is perfectly content to spend her days lying at my feet.

Angel is such a perfect baby that I love taking pictures of her, and I always want to share them with everyone. It's okay if you bore your friends and relatives with pictures of your children, but once you start showing pictures of your puppy, most people's eyes glaze over.

That's when I decided to put my puppy's pictures in a quilt! (I even found room for a few pictures of her brother and her father.) I used the program Kaleidoscope Kreator™ 2.0 to make the 8-point stars. Then the stars are cut out and appliquéd to background squares. I also give instructions for making the stars without the program.

Looking at the quilt, only the most discerning can see that the design inside the stars is made with a puppy's face. For those who don't like looking at puppy pictures, it's just a wonderful design.

—Linda Causee

My Puppy's Pictures

Approximate Size: 50" x 60"

Materials

20 photos at least 3" x 5"
1 1/2 yards white paw prints
2 1/4 yards red paw print (including binding)
2 1/2 yards black dog bone print (blocks, border)
3 yards backing
batting
*40 prepared fabric sheets
 *Purchase prepared fabric sheets or refer to Preparing Your
 Own Fabric for Printing, page 121, to make your own.
sewing needle and thread
template plastic

Pattern (page 97)

Kite Template

Cutting

Blocks

20 squares, 8 1/2" x 8 1/2", black dog bone print
8 kite shapes from each photo (see instructions below)

Finishing

6 strips, 2 1/2"-wide, red paw print
6 strips, 2 1/2"-wide, white paw print
31 strips, 2 1/2" x 8 1/2", white paw print
18 strips, 2 1/2" x 8 1/2", red paw print
12 squares, 2 1/2" x 2 1/2", red paw print
6 strips, 4 1/2"-wide, black dog bone print (border)
6 strips, 2 1/2"-wide, red paw print (binding)

Instructions

Preparation

1. If making your own fabric sheets, read Preparing Fabric for Printing, page 121.

2. Make a see-through plastic Kite template by tracing the Kite pattern from page 97 onto template plastic.

3. Make four copies of each photograph that you are using for your quilt.

Making the Blocks

1. Starting with the first set of photos, place the Kite template on top of one photograph to get the best position possible for the Kaleidoscope. (**Diagram 1**) Trace the kite shape on the photograph and cut out along drawn line. Cut kite shape from remaining three photos.

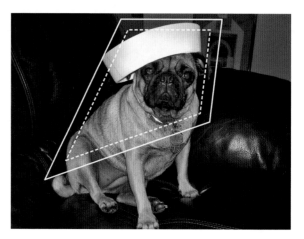

1

2. Position the four kite photographs on copier or computer scanner. You will be able to fit four kite photos on each fabric sheet. Copy or scan directly onto fabric sheets; repeat. You will need eight fabric copies of EACH photograph. **Note:** *Be sure to use the appropriate settings for your printer or copier.*

3. Cut the kite photographs from the fabric sheets.

4. Repeat steps for all photos.

5. Working with one group at a time, sew photo kites in pairs along longest side. Press seams open. (**Diagram 2**) You will have four pairs for each block.

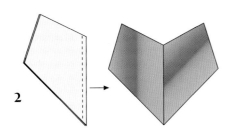

6. Sew pairs together to make half of block. Press seams open. (**Diagram 3**)

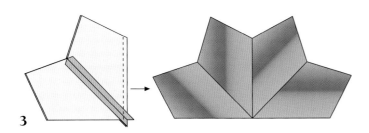

7. Sew halves together to complete star. Press seam open. (**Diagram 4**) Press outer raw edges under ¹/4".

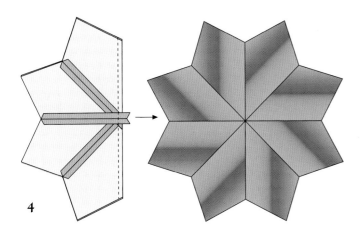

8. Center star on 8¹/2"" x 8¹/2"" black print square. (**Diagram 5**)

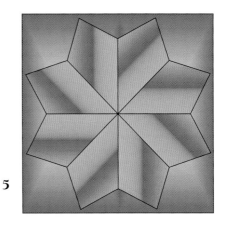

9. Using a small machine zigzag, sew along outside edge of star to complete block.

10. Repeat steps 5-9 for remaining blocks.

Finishing

1. Sew a red paw print strip and a white paw print strip together lengthwise. Press seam toward red strip. Repeat for five more strip sets. (**Diagram 6**)

2. Cut strip sets into 8½" intervals for a total of 18 pairs of rectangles. (**Diagram 7**)

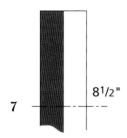

7   8½"

3. Cut remaining strip sets into 2½" intervals for a total of 22 pairs of squares. (**Diagram 8**)

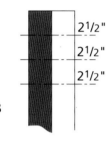

8   2½"
      2½"
      2½"

4. Sew two pairs of squares for form a nine patch. Make four nine patches for corners of quilt. (**Diagram 9**)

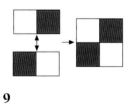

9

5. Place blocks in five rows of four blocks. Place sashing strips and cornerstones in between and pairs of sashing strips and squares along outside edges. Sew blocks and sashing rows. Sew sashing and cornerstone rows; press seams to left. (**Diagram 10**)

6. Sew rows together.

7. Measure quilt top lengthwise.

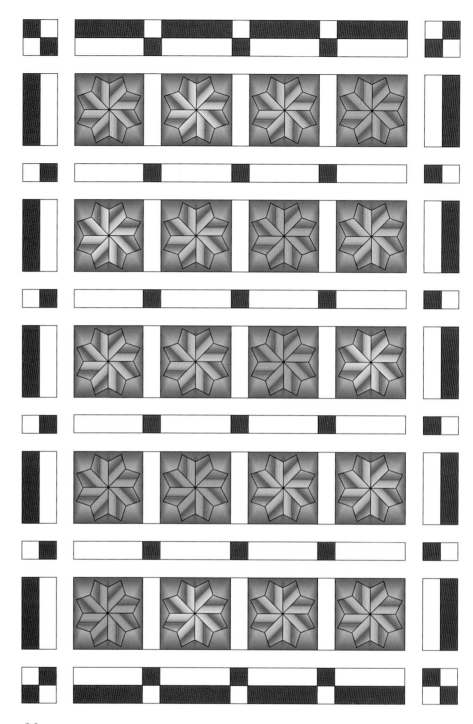

10

Piece and cut two 4½"-wide black dog bone strips. Sew to sides of quilt. Measure quilt top crosswise. Piece and cut two strips to the length. Sew to top and bottom of quilt.

8. Refer to Finishing Your Quilt, pages 123 to 127, to complete your quilt.

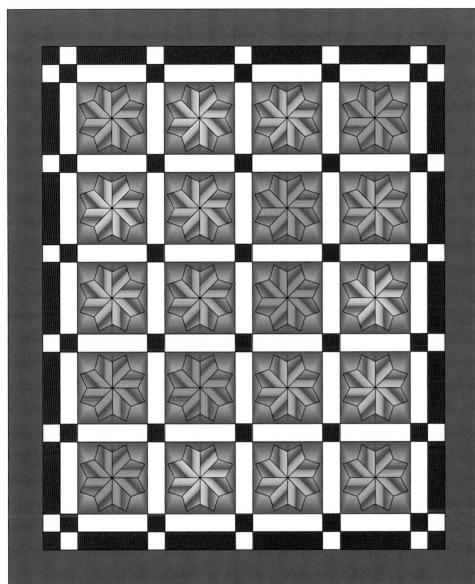

My Puppy's Pictures Quilt Layout

"It's okay if you bore your friends and relatives with pictures of your children, but once you start showing pictures of your puppy, most people's eyes glaze over....That's when I decided to put my puppy's pictures in a quilt!"

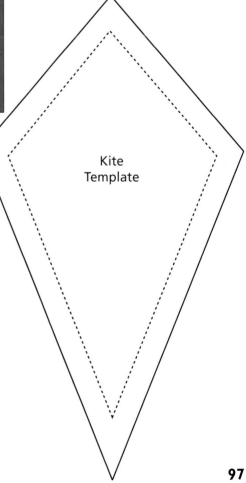

Kite Template

Optional

Making Blocks with Kaleidoscope Kreator™ 2.0

Use the Kaleidoscope Kreator™ 2.0 program, following manufacturer's directions, to create the Kaleidoscope blocks on your computer.

Print the blocks onto fabric using prepared fabric sheets.

Cut out kaleidoscope star.

Center kaleidoscope star on 8¹/2" x 8¹/2" black dog bone print square. Using a small machine zigzag, sew along outside edge of star along outside edge to complete block. Repeat for remaining blocks.

Tickets Please

by Rita Weiss

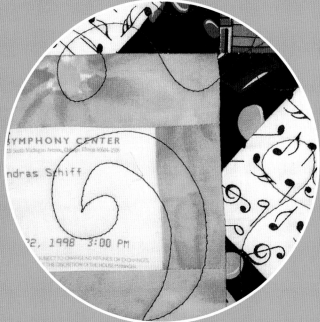

I thought I was the only person who collected bits and pieces which slept in boxes and drawers. I've now discovered it is a universal disease.

When we were discussing this book with Joyce Lerner, who was to handle the graphics on the book, she admitted to her own collection. A music lover, she collects the tickets of every concert she has ever attended.

Of course, I had no choice but make a quilt for Joyce, using fabrics with musical themes to hold the entire collection together, and using fanciful G-clefs as the quilting motifs.

While I was working on the quilt, one ticket brought back a flood of memories to me. It was for a recital at the Aspen Music Festival in Colorado over ten years ago given by the famous pianist Mitsuko Uchida. I was there with Joyce!

But, what was more exciting for us was the day after the concert when walking along the street in downtown Aspen, we met the pianist herself. We stopped to tell her how much we loved her and her concert. She was more than gracious, and she took the time to explain her theories on concertizing with us. Of course, she was a favorite before the concert, but now she occupies a special place in the all-time greats. What a great memory that we can both now share!

Maybe there's something to this collecting business after all.

Once I had finished with the quilt, Joyce asked me to be sure and return her tickets. The quilt may be superb, but there is something about the real thing...I guess.

—*Rita Weiss*

Tickets Please

Approximate Size: 51" x 55"

Materials

1 1/2 yards black music print (includes border)

1 1/2 yards white music print

1 1/4 yards black keyboard print (includes binding)

1 1/2 yards total, assorted colors

3 yards backing

batting

35 ticket stubs

*12 prepared fabric sheets

*Purchase prepared fabric sheets or refer to Preparing Your Own Fabric for Printing, page 121, to make your own.

Cutting

Blocks

280 squares, 2" x 2", black music print

70 rectangles, 2" x 6 1/2", white music print

70 rectangles, 2" x 4 1/2", white music print

140 squares, 2" x 2", black keyboard print

18-20 strips, 2"-wide, assorted colors

Finishing

6 strips, 3 1/2"-wide, black music print (border)

6 strips, 2 1/2"-wide, black keyboard print (binding)

Instructions

1. Referring to Printing Photos to Fabric, pages 121 to 122, print ticket stubs onto fabric sheets spacing stubs at least 1/2" apart. You should be able to get three ticket stubs on each sheet.

2. Cut out ticket stubs 1/4" from all edges.

3. Place ticket stub right sides together with a 2"-wide colored strip; sew with a 1/4" seam allowance. (**Diagram 1**)

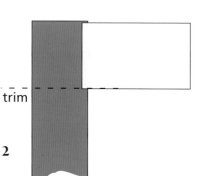

4. Fold strip open and trim strip even with ticket stub. (**Diagram 2**)

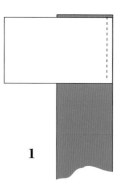

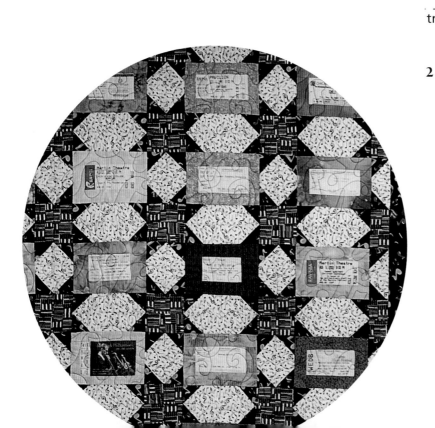

5. Repeat step 3 on opposite side of ticket stub; (**Diagram 3**)

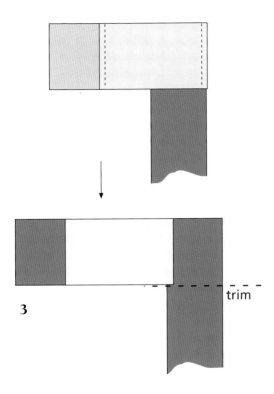

3

trim

6. Repeat on remaining two edges. Trim block to 4¹/2" x 6¹/2". (**Diagram 4**) Repeat steps 3 to 6 for all printed ticket stubs.

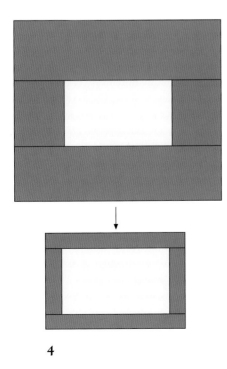

4

7. Place 2" black music print square right sides together with 2" x 4¹/2" white music print rectangle. Sew diagonally from corner to corner of black square. (**Diagram 5**) **Hint:** *Draw a diagonal line on wrong side of each black music square.*

5

8. Trim ¹/4" from sewing line and fold resulting triangle back. (**Diagram 6**)

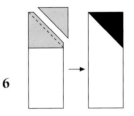

6

9. Repeat on opposite side of white music print rectangle. (**Diagram 7**)

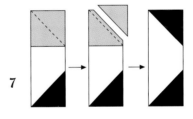

7

10. Repeat steps 7 to 9 for remaining 2" x 4¹/2" white music print rectangles.

11. Sew resulting strips to opposite sides of framed ticket stubs. (**Diagram 8**)

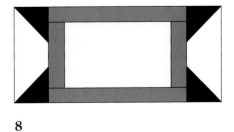

8

12. Repeat steps 8 to 10 using 2" x 6½" white music print rectangles and 2" black music print squares. (**Diagram 9**)

9

13. Sew a 2" black keyboard print square to each end of strips made in step 13. (**Diagram 10**)

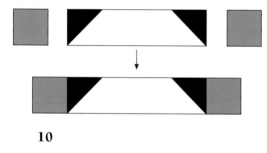

10

14. Sew resulting strips to top and bottom to complete blocks. (**Diagram 11**)

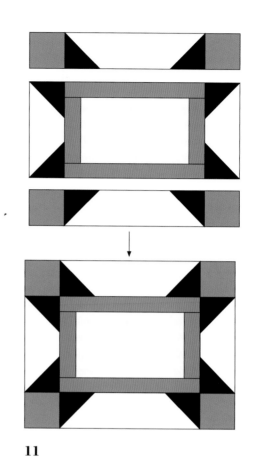

11

Finishing

1. Place blocks in seven rows of five blocks. Sew together in rows, then sew rows together.

2. Measure quilt lengthwise; piece and cut two 3½"-wide black music print strips to that length. Sew to sides of quilt. Measure quilt crosswise; piece and cut two 3½"-wide black music print strips to that length. Sew to top and bottom of quilt.

3. Refer to Finishing Your Quilt, pages 123 to 127, to complete your quilt.

Tickets Please Quilt Layout

"What a great memory that we can both
now share! Maybe there's something to this
collecting business after all."

T-Shirt Memories

by Linda Causee

My son—like many of us—loves T-shirts. Wherever he went he was always sure to arrive back home with a T-shirt to commemorate the moment.

His collection of T-shirts from his junior high school days through his high school and college graduation filled several drawers in his bedroom dresser. It was time to clean house and certainly time to do something with the T-shirts.

I just couldn't throw out a T-shirt awarded in high school for outstanding behavior, or a T-shirt from the marching band or the wrestling team. How can you throw out a T-shirt from an international karate tournament with members from Russia?

I had the answer. You don't throw out the shirts, you put them together into a quilt.

The shirts were cut up and made into smaller T-shirt blocks for the quilt. To fit more shirts into the quilt, the blocks face both up and down: the shirts that are upside down fit under the arms of the shirts that are right side up.

When my son first saw the quilt, he was aghast that I had cut up his T-shirt collection. Then he realized that now he could "wear" all of his shirts at the same time. So long as he has his quilt, he has all the memories he needs.

—Linda Causee

T-shirt Memories

Approximate Size: 92" x 118"

Materials

assorted T-shirts
   (the photographed quilt uses 35 t-shirts)
9-10 yards medium-weight fusible interfacing
$1^1/4$ yards dark blue print (border)
$3/4$ yard binding
8 yards backing
king size batting

Cutting

Blocks

25 rectangles, $15^1/2$" x $17^1/2$", fusible interfacing
   (T-shirt block)
10 rectangles, $8^1/2$" x $17^1/2$", fusible interfacing
   (partial block)
60 rectangles, 8" x 7", fusible interfacing (sleeves)

Finishing

10 strips, $4^1/2$"-wide, dark blue print (border)
10 strips, $2^1/2$"-wide, binding

Working with T-shirts

• The T-shirt blocks for the photographed quilt were cut $14^1/2$" x $16^1/2$"; the partial blocks for the sides of the quilt were cut $7^1/2$" x $16^1/2$" and the sleeve rectangles were cut $7^1/2$" x $6^1/2$". If your T-shirts are not large enough to cut $14^1/2$" x $16^1/2$" rectangles, you can cut the T-shirt blocks, partial blocks and sleeve rectangles according to the following measurements:

T-shirt blocks	Partial blocks	Sleeves	Quilt Size
$12^1/2$" x $14^1/2$"	$6^1/2$" x $14^1/2$"	$6^1/2$" x $5^1/2$"	72" x 95"
$10^1/2$" x $12^1/2$"	$5^1/2$" x $12^1/2$"	$5^1/2$" x $4^1/2$"	60" x 80"
$8^1/2$" x $10^1/2$"	$4^1/2$" x $10^1/2$"	$4^1/2$" x $3^1/2$"	48" x 65"

• Look at the designs on your chosen T-shirts. Use the largest as the guide for cutting all blocks.

• Since T-shirts are made from stretchy knit fabric, interfacing must be fused to the wrong side of the T-shirt fabric. Lift iron up and down rather than side to side to avoid wrinkles being formed.

• Cut off sleeves, then cut away front of T-shirt at shoulders and down each side.

• Use T-shirts with small logos for the partial blocks.

• Use the sleeves of the T-shirts to cut the sleeve rectangles. If the sleeves are not large enough, use the backs of the T-shirts.

• If you don't have enough T-shirts, you can use the backs to cut additional rectangles to $6^1/2$" x $7^1/2$". You should have two small rectangles for each large rectangle.

Instructions

1. Press shirt front, then place shirt front right side down on ironing board; center $15^1/2$" x $17^1/2$" interfacing rectangle over design and press to fuse. (**Diagram 1**)

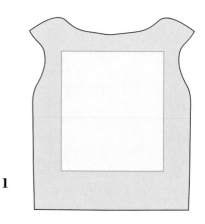

1

2. Trim shirt so block measures $14^1/2$" x $16^1/2$".

3. Repeat steps 1 and 2 for remaining shirts.

4. For partial blocks, position $8^1/2$" x $17^1/2$" interfacing so a small logo is centered about 3" below top of interfacing; fuse in place. Trim partial block to $7^1/2$" x $16^1/2$".
Note: *If you do not have a T-shirt with a small logo, use the backs of shirts already used.*

5. Using the backs of the T-shirts (or sleeves if large enough), place two 8" x 7" interfacing rectangles on wrong side of each back. Fuse interfacing to fabric following manufacturer's instructions. Trim rectangles to $6^1/2$" x $7^1/2$". You should have two sleeve rectangles for each T-shirt block and one sleeve rectangle for each partial block.

6. Place large full rectangles, partial rectangles, and small rectangles referring to photograph and quilt layout. Be sure to note placement of small rectangles in relation to the large full and partial rectangles. The quilt top should look like T-shirts with adjacent rows going in opposite directions. (**Diagram 2**)

2

"I just couldn't throw out a
T-shirt awarded in high school for
outstanding behavior, or a T-shirt
from the marching band or the
wrestling team."

6. Sew large rectangles to sleeve rectangles being sure to keep them in the correct order. (**Diagram 3**)

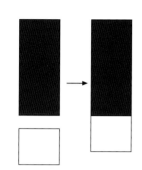

3

7. Sew adjacent sleeve rectangles in pairs, then sew to the corresponding T-shirt block. (**Diagram 4**) Repeat for all rectangles.

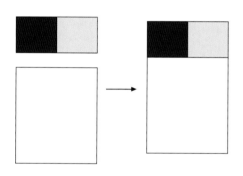

4

8. Sew units made in steps 6 and 7 in rows, then sew rows together. (**Diagram 5**)

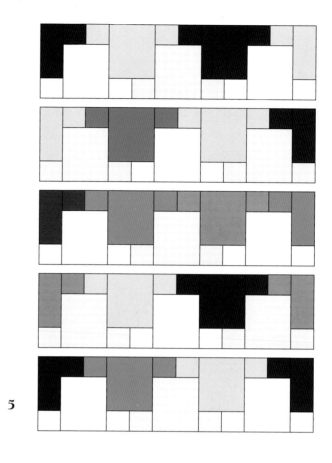

5

9. Measure quilt lengthwise. Sew and cut two 4 1/2"-wide dark blue strips to that length. Sew to sides of quilt. Measure quilt crosswise. Sew and cut two 4 1/2"-wide dark blue strips to that length and sew to top and bottom of quilt.

10. Refer to Finishing Your Quilt, pages 123 to 127, to complete your quilt.

T-Shirt Memories Quilt Layout

"...he was always sure to arrive back home

with a T-shirt to commemorate the moment."

General Directions

Fabric

For over a hundred years, quilts have been made with 100% cotton fabric, the choice for most quilters.

There are many properties in cotton that make it especially well-suited to quilt making. There is less distortion in cotton fabric, thereby affording the quilter greater security in making certain that even the smallest bits of fabric will fit together. Because a quilt block made of cotton can be ironed flat with a steam iron, a puckered area, created by mistake, can be fixed. The sewing machine needle can move through cotton with a great deal of ease when compared to some synthetic fabrics. While you may find that quilt artists today often use other kinds of fabric, to create the quilts quickly and accurately, 100% cotton is strongly recommended.

Cotton fabric today is produced in so many wonderful and exciting combinations of prints and solids that it is often difficult to pick colors for your quilt. We've chosen our favorite colors for these quilts, but don't be afraid to make your own choices

For years, quilters were advised to prewash all of their fabric to test for colorfastness and shrinkage. Now most quilters don't bother to prewash all of their fabric but they do pretest it. Cut a strip about 2" wide from each piece of fabric that you will use in your quilt. Measure both the length and the width of the strip. Then immerse it in a bowl of very hot water, using a separate bowl for each piece of fabric. Be especially concerned about reds and dark blues because they have a tendency to bleed if the initial dyeing was not done properly. If it's one of your favorite fabrics that's bleeding, you might be able to salvage the fabric. Try washing the fabric in very hot water until you've washed out all of the excess dye. Unfortunately, fabrics that continue to bleed after they have been washed repeatedly will bleed forever. So eliminate them right at the start.

Now, take the strips and iron them dry with a hot iron. Be especially careful not to stretch the strip. When the strips are completely dry, measure and compare them to your original strip. If all of your fabric is shrinking the same amount, you don't have to worry about uneven shrinkage in your quilt. When you wash the final quilt, the puckering that will result may give you the look of an antique quilt. If you don't want this look, you are going to have to wash and dry all of your fabric before you start cutting. Iron the fabric using some spray starch or sizing to give the fabric a crisp finish.

If you are never planning to wash your quilt, i.e. your quilt is intended to be a wall hanging such as many of the quilts in this collection, you could eliminate the pre-testing process. You may run the risk, however, of some future relative to whom you have willed your quilts deciding that the wall hanging needs freshening by washing.

Before beginning to work, make sure that your fabric is absolutely square. If it is not, you will have difficulty cutting square pieces. Fabric is woven with crosswise and lengthwise threads. Lengthwise threads should be parallel to the selvage (that's the finished edge along the sides; sometimes the fabric company prints its name along the selvage), and crosswise threads should be perpendicular to the selvage. If fabric is off grain, you can usually straighten it by pulling gently on the true bias in the opposite direction to the off-grain edge. Continue doing this until the crosswise threads are at a right angle to the lengthwise threads.

Rotary Cutting

Supplies for Rotary Cutting

For rotary cutting, you will need three important tools: a rotary cutter, a mat and an acrylic ruler. There are currently on the market many different brands and types. Choose the kinds that you feel will work for you. Ask your quilting friends what their preferences are, then make your decision.

There are several different rotary cutters now available with special features that you might prefer such as the type of handle, whether the cutter can be used for both right- and left-handed quilters, safety features, size, and finally the cost.

Don't attempt to use the rotary cutter without an accompanying protective mat. The mat will not only protect your table from becoming scratched, but it will protect your cutter as well. The mat is self-healing and will not dull the cutting blades. Mats are available in many sizes, but if this is your first attempt at rotary cutting, an 18" x 24" mat is probably your best choice. When you are not using your mat, be sure to store it on a flat surface. Otherwise your mat will bend. If you want to keep your mat from warping, make certain that it is not sitting in direct sunlight; the heat can cause the mat to warp. You will not be able to cut accurately if you use a bent or warped mat.

Another must for cutting accurate strips is a strong straight edge. Acrylic rulers are the perfect choice for this. There are many different brands of acrylic rulers on the market, and they come in several widths and lengths. Either a 6" x 24" or a 6" x 12" ruler will be the most useful. The longer ruler will allow you to fold your fabric only once while the smaller size will require folding the fabric twice. Make sure that your ruler has 1/8" increment markings in both directions plus a 45-degree marking.

Cutting Strips With a Rotary Cutter.

Before beginning to work, iron your fabric to remove the wrinkles. Fold the fabric in half, lengthwise, bringing the selvage edges together. Fold in half again. Make sure that there are no wrinkles in the fabric.

Now place the folded fabric on the cutting mat. Place the fabric length on the right side if you are right-handed or on the left side if you are left-handed. (**Diagram 1**) The fold of the fabric should line up along one of the grid lines printed on the mat.

right handed

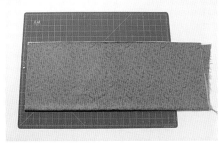

left handed

1

Straighten one of the cut edges first. Lay the acrylic ruler on the mat near the cut edge; the ruler markings should be even with the grid on the mat. Hold the ruler firmly with your left hand (or, with your right hand if you are left-handed). To provide extra stability, keep your small finger off the mat. Now hold the rotary cutter with blade against the ruler and cut away from you in one quick motion. (**Diagram 2**)

2

Carefully turn the fabric (or mat with the fabric) so the straightened edge is on the opposite side. Place the ruler on the required width line along the cut edge of the fabric and cut the strip, making sure that you always cut away from you—never toward you. Cut the number of strips called for in the directions. (**Diagram 3**)

3

After you have cut a few strips, you will want to check to make certain that your fabric continues to be perfectly square. To do this, just line up the crosswise markings along the folded edge of fabric and the lengthwise edge of the ruler next to the end of fabric you are cutting. Cut off uneven edge. If you fail to do this, your strips may be bowed with a "v" in the center, causing your piecing to become inaccurate as you continue working.

Cutting Squares and Rectangles

Now that you have cut your strips, you can begin to cut squares or rectangles. Place a stack of strips on the cutting mat. You will be more successful in cutting—at least in the beginning—if you work with no more than four strips at a time. Make certain that the strips are lined up very evenly. Following the instructions given for the quilt, cut the required number of squares or rectangles. (**Diagram 4**)

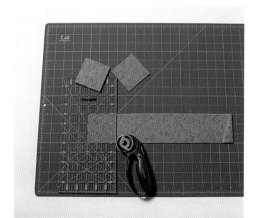

4

Cutting Triangles

Once your squares are cut, you can cut triangles, including half-square triangles and triangle squares.

Half-Square Triangles

The short sides of a half-square triangle are on the short grain of the fabric. This is especially necessary if the short edges are on the outer side of the block.

Cut the squares the size indicated in the instructions, then cut the square in half diagonally. (**Diagram 5**).

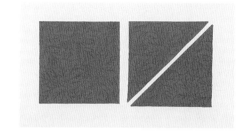

5

Triangle Squares

These are squares made up of two different-colored triangles. To make these squares, you can cut individual triangles as described in Half-Square Triangles above. Then sew two triangles together. A quick method, especially if you have several triangle squares with the same fabric, is to sew two squares together. Then draw a diagonal line on the wrong side of the lighter square. Place two squares right sides together and sew 1/4" from each side of the drawn line.

Cut along the drawn line, and you have created two triangle squares. (**Diagram 6**)

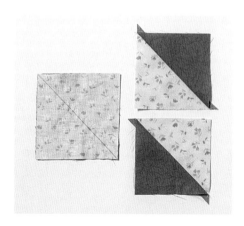

6

Stitch and Flip

This is a method for quickly creating triangles and octagons or trapezoids.

Instead of cutting these shapes, you cut and sew squares or rectangles together. (**Diagram 7**)

7

With right sides together, place a small square in the corner of a larger square or rectangle. You then sew diagonally from corner to corner of the small square. (**Diagram 8**)

8

Trim the corner about 1/4" from the seam line. (**Diagram 9**)

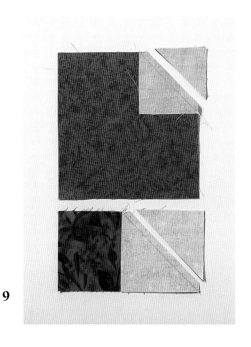

9

Flip the triangle over and press. (**Diagram 10**)

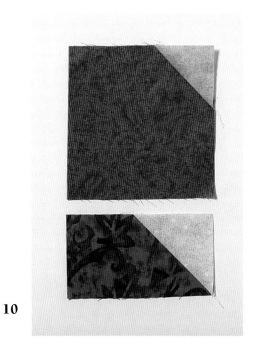

10

Repeat at the other corners. (**Diagram 11**)

11

Strip Piecing

Strip piecing is a much faster and easier method of making quilts rather than creating the blocks piece by piece. With this method, two or more strips are sewn together and then cut at certain intervals. For instance, if a block is made up of several 3" finished squares, cut 3$^{1}/_{2}$"-wide strips along the crosswise grain, (**Diagram 12**)

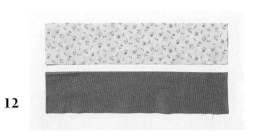

12

With right sides together, sew two strips along the length. The seam should be pressed across the dark side of the fabric (**Diagram 13**).

13

Cut across strips at 3$^{1}/_{2}$" intervals to create pairs of 3$^{1}/_{2}$" squares. (**Diagram 14**)

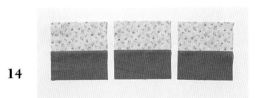

14

Foundation Piecing

One of the easiest and most accurate methods for creating perfect quilt squares is Foundation Piecing.

Materials

Before you begin, decide the kind of foundation on which you are planning to piece the blocks.

Paper

The most popular choice is paper. It's readily available and fairly inexpensive. You can use copy paper, newsprint, tracing paper—even computer paper. The paper does not remain a permanent part of your quilt as it is removed once the blocks are completely sewn.

Fabric

If you choose to hand piece your block, you may want to choose fabric as your foundation. Just remember that fabric is not removed after you make your block so you will have another layer to quilt through. This may be a problem if you are planning to hand quilt. Using fabric might be an advantage, however, if you want to use some non-traditional quilting fabrics, such as silk or satin, since the fabric foundation will add stability to the block. Fabric makes a good choice for crazy quilts. If you do decide to use fabric, choose a lightweight and light-colored fabric, such as muslin, that will allow you to see through for ease in tracing.

Other Materials

Another option for foundation materials is Tear Away™ or Fun-dation™, translucent non-woven materials combining both the advantages of both paper and fabric. They are easy to see through, but like paper they can be removed with ease.

Currently a new kind of foundation material has appeared in the market place: a foundation paper that dissolves in water after use. Two companies, W.H. Collins and EZ Quilting by Wrights are producing this product.

Preparing the Foundation

Place your foundation material over your chosen block and trace the block pattern. Use a ruler and a fine-line pencil or permanent marker, and make sure that all lines are straight. Sometimes short dashed lines or even dotted lines are easier to make. Be sure to copy all numbers. You will need to make a foundation for each block you are planning to use.

If you have a home copier, you can copy your tracing on the copy machine. Since the copy machine might slightly alter the measurements of the block, make certain that you copy each block from the original pattern.

You can also scan the block if you have a home scanner and then print out the required number of blocks.

Cutting the Fabric

In foundation piecing, you do not have to cut perfect shapes!

You can, therefore, use odd pieces of fabric: squares, strips, rectangles. The one thing you must remember, however, is that every piece must be at least 1/4" larger on all sides than the space it is going to cover. Strips and squares are easy: just measure the length and width of the needed space and add 1/2" all around. Cut your strip to that measurement. Triangles, however, can be a bit tricky. In that case, measure the widest point of the triangle and cut your fabric about 1/2" to 1" wider.

Other Supplies for Foundation Piecing

Piecing by hand:
You will need a reasonably thin needle such as a Sharp size 10; a good-quality, neutral-colored thread such as a size 50 cotton; some pins, a glue stick; fabric scissors; muslin or fabric for the bases.

Piecing by machine:
You will need a cleaned and oiled sewing machine; glue stick; pins, paper scissors, fabric scissors, foundation material.

Before beginning to sew your actual block by machine, determine the proper stitch length. Use a piece of the paper you are planning to use for the foundation and draw a straight line on it. Set your machine so that it sews with a fairly short stitch (about 20 stitches per inch). Sew along the line. If you can tear the paper apart with ease, you are sewing with the right length. You don't want to sew with such a short stitch that the paper falls apart by itself. If you are going to use a fabric foundation with the sewing machine, use the stitch length you normally use since you won't be removing the fabric foundation.

Using a Pattern

The numbers on the block show the order in which the pieces are to be placed and sewn on the base.

It is extremely important that you follow the numbers; otherwise the entire process won't work.

Making the Block

The important thing to remember about making a foundation block is that the fabric pieces go on the unmarked side of the foundation while you sew on the printed side. The finished blocks are a mirror image of the original pattern.

Step 1:
Hold the foundation up to a light source - even a window pane—with the unmarked side facing. Find the space marked 1 on the unmarked side and put a dab of glue there. Place the fabric right side up on the unmarked side on Space 1, making certain that the fabric overlaps at least 1/4" on all sides of space 1. (**Diagram 15**)

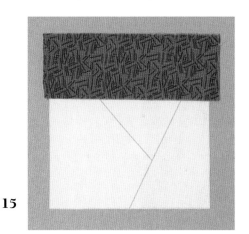

15

Step 2:
Fold the foundation along the line between Space 1 and Space 2. Cut the fabric so that it is 1/4" from the fold. (**Diagram 16**)

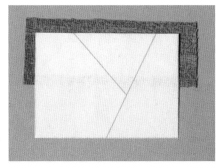

16

Step 3:
With right sides together, place Fabric Piece 2 on Fabric Piece 1, making sure that the edge of Piece 2 is even with the just-trimmed edge of Piece 1. (**Diagram 17**)

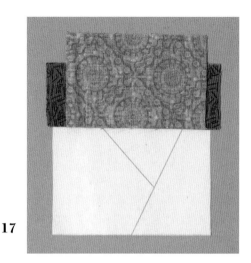

17

Step 4:
To make certain that Piece 2 will cover Space 2, fold the fabric piece back along the line between Space 1 and Space 2. (**Diagram 18**)

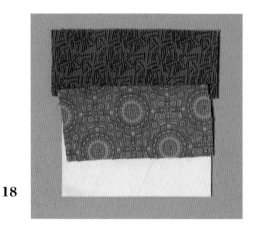

18

Step 5:
With the marked side of the foundation facing up, place the piece on the sewing machine (or sew by hand), holding both Piece 1 and Piece 2 in place. Sew along the line between Space 1 and Space 2. (**Diagram 19**)

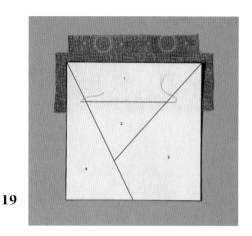

19

If you use a small stitch, it will be easier to remove the paper later. Start sewing about two or three stitches before the beginning of the line and end your sewing two or three stitches beyond the line. This will allow the stitching to be held in place by the next round of stitching rather than by backstitching.

Step 6:
Turn the work over and open Piece 2. Finger press the seam open. (**Diagram 20**)

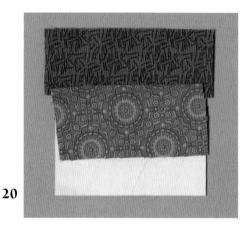

20

Step 7:
Turning the work so that the marked side is on top, fold the foundation forward along the line between Space 1+2 and Space 3. Trim about 1/8" to 1/4" from the fold. It is easier to trim the paper if you pull the paper away from the stitching. If you use fabric as your foundation, fold the fabric forward as far as it will go and then start to trim. (**Diagram 21**)

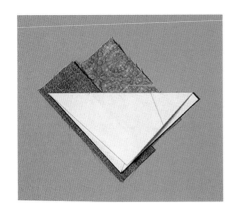

21

Step 8:
Place Fabric #3 right side down even with the just-trimmed edge. (**Diagram 22**)

22

Step 9:
Turn the block over to the marked side and sew along the line between Space 1+2 and Space 3. (**Diagram 23**)

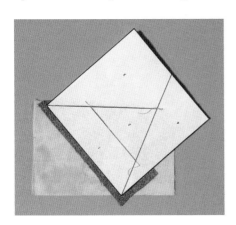

23

Step 10:
Turn the work over, open Piece 3 and finger press the seam. (**Diagram 24**)

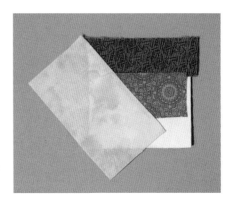

24

Step 11:
In the same way you have added the other pieces, add Piece #4 to complete this block. Trim the fabric 1/4" from the edge of the foundation. The foundation-pieced block is completed. (**Diagram 25**)

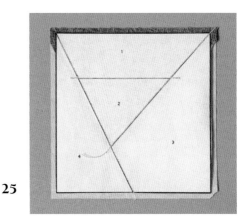

25

After you have finished sewing a block, don't immediately remove the paper. Since you are often piecing with tiny bits of fabric, grainline is never a factor. Therefore, some of the pieces may have been cut on the bias and may have a tendency to stretch. You can eliminate any problem with distortion by keeping the paper in place until all of the blocks have been sewn together. If, however, you want to remove the paper, stay stitch along the outer edge of the block to help keep the block in shape.

Sewing Multiple Sections

Some blocks in foundation piecing, such as the Mailbox block in Postcards, are created with two or more sections. These sections, which are indicated by letters, are individually pieced and then sewn together. The cutting line for these sections is indicated by a bold line. Before you start to make any of these multi-section blocks, begin by cutting the foundation piece apart so that each section is worked independently. Leave a 1/4" seam allowance around each section.

Step 1:
Following the instructions above for Making the Block, complete each section. Then place the sections right side together. Pin the corners of the top section to the corners of the bottom section. (**Diagram 26**)

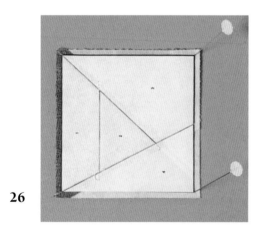

26

Step 2:
If you are certain that the pieces are aligned correctly, sew the two sections together using the regular stitch length on the sewing machine. (**Diagram 27**)

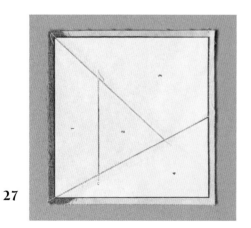

27

Step 3:
Press the sections open and continue sewing the sections in pairs. (**Diagram 28**)

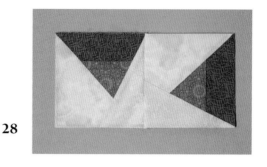

28

Step 4:
Sew necessary pairs of sections together to complete the block. (**Diagram 29**)

29

The blocks are now ready to sew into your quilts.

What You Don't Want to Forget

1. If you plan to sew by hand, begin by taking some backstitches which will anchor the thread at the beginning of the line. Then use a backstitch every four or five stitches. End the stitching with a few backstitches.

2. If you plan to sew by machine, start stitching two or three stitches before the start of the stitching line and finish your stitching two or three stitches beyond the end.

3. Use a short stitch (about 20 stitches per inch) for paper foundations to make it easier to remove the paper. If the paper falls apart as you sew, your stitches are too short.

4. Finger press (or use an iron) each seam as you finish it.

5. Stitching which goes from a space into another space will not interfere with adding additional fabric pieces.

6. Remember to trim all seam allowances at least 1/4".

7. When sewing points, start from the wide end and sew towards the point.

8. Unless you plan to use it only once in the block, it is a good idea to stay away from directional prints in foundation piecing.

9. When cutting pieces for foundation piecing, never worry about the grainline.

10. Always remember to sew on the marked side, placing the fabric on the unmarked side.

11. Follow the numerical order, or it won't work.

12. Once you have finished making a block, do not remove the paper until the entire quilt has been finished unless you stay stitch around the outside of the block.

13. Be sure that the ink you use to make your foundation is permanent and will not wash out into your fabric.

Easy Applique

Using Paper-backed Fusible Web

Appliquéing with paper-backed fusible web is an easy and quick way to attach fabric shapes to a background fabric. Use a lightweight product so that your needle does not get gummed up when machine sewing the edges.

Step 1:
Trace pattern onto the paper side of the fusible web. Rough cut pattern shape.

Step 2:
Position fusible web pattern with paper side up onto wrong side of fabric; fuse in place with hot iron. **Note:** *Refer to manufacturer's directions for heating setting and pressing time for the product you are using. Cut out along drawn line. Repeat for all patterns.*

Step 3:
Position fusible appliqué pieces onto background fabric as shown in the project instructions. Fuse into place following manufacturer's instructions.

Step 4:
Using a machine zigzag stitch and matching or invisible thread, stitch along all raw edges of appliqué pieces. **Hint:** *Practice on another piece of fabric to see which zigzag width and length works best for you.*

Appliqué with Fusible Interfacing

Appliquéing with fusible interfacing gives pieces with raw edges that are turned under. The pieces can be positioned, then fused in place making the appliqué process easier and quicker whether you appliqué by hand or machine.

You will need template plastic and lightweight fusible interfacing.

Step 1:
Trace patterns onto clear template plastic. Cut out along drawn line.

Step 2:
Place template on wrong side of fabric. Draw along outside edge using a pencil or a removable fabric marker. Cut out fabric about 1/4" from drawn line. (**Diagram 30**)

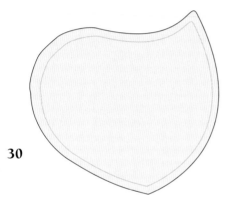

30

Step 3:
Rough cut a piece of lightweight fusible interfacing that is slightly larger than the fabric appliqué. **Note:** *You don't have to cut the interfacing the exact shape of the fabric appliqué at this time.* (**Diagram 31**)

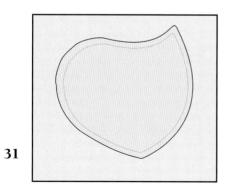

31

Step 4:
Place fabric appliqué right side together with bumpy (fusible) side of interfacing. Sew along entire drawn line of fabric appliqué. (**Diagram 32**)

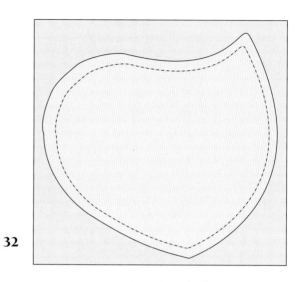

32

Step 5:
Make a small slit through interfacing being careful not to catch fabric with scissors. (**Diagram 33**) Trim interfacing even with fabric edge.

33

Step 6:
Turn fabric appliqué right side out through opening. Use a blunt, pointed tool such as a knitting needle to shape edges at seam. Place appliqué on a flat surface and finger press along outer edges. Appliqué piece is now ready to be fused to background fabric.

Printing Photos to Fabric

Purchased Fabric Sheets

By far the easiest method for transferring photos onto fabric is to purchase prepared fabric sheets at your local quilt shop. There are several on the market: June Tailor Colorfast Computer Printer Fabric (white or cream); Printed Treasures fabric sheets; and Inkjet Transfer Paper by TransferMagic.com. Just download your digital photos onto your computer or scan printed photos. Then re-size the photos to fit the project and print onto the fabric sheets following the manufacturer's directions.

Preparing Your Own Fabric for Printing

Although purchased fabric sheets are easy to use, they can be very costly especially if you have several items to print onto fabric. To prepare your fabric for printing, you will need high-quality 100% cotton fabric, Bubble Jet Set 2000, square plastic tub, rubber gloves, freezer paper, rotary cutter, mat and ruler, and Bubble Jet Rinse.
Note: *Bubble Jet Set 2000 and Bubble Jet Rinse can be purchased at your local quilt shop.*

Step 1:

Use high quality 100% cotton such as Kona Cotton by Robert Kaufmann. The fabric should be at least 200 threads per inch. Cut the fabric into rectangles, 9" x 11½" which is slightly larger than a sheet of paper.

Step 2:

Pour a little of the Bubble Jet Set 2000 into a square plastic tub. The Bubble Jet Set will allow the ink of your inkjet printer to bond permanently with your fabric.

Step 3:

Place a fabric rectangle into the plastic tub. Wearing a pair of rubber gloves, push the fabric into the liquid until it is soaked through. Add another fabric rectangle, add a little more Bubble Jet set 2000 and thoroughly saturate the fabric. Continue this process until you have treated all the fabric needed for your project.

Step 4:

Let the fabric air dry by hanging or lay the fabric on a table covered with plastic. Pour any leftover Bubble Jet Set liquid back into the bottle for the next use.

Step 5:

When the fabric rectangles are completely dry, iron to the shiny side of freezer paper. Be sure that there are no air bubbles between the fabric and freezer paper. Also, do not overheat the fabric and freezer paper or you will lose the bonding ability.

Step 6:

Trim the sheets to 8½" x 11". Be sure to use a sharp rotary cutter. Trim any loose threads hanging from the fabric edges.

Step 7:

Change your printer settings to the highest DPI and the media type setting to high gloss photo paper. Print photos.

Step 8:

Let the printed pages set at least 24 hours then rinse with Bubble Jet Set Rinse. The rinsing step is important because it removes excess ink so the pictures don't run during subsequent washings. You do not need to heat set with an iron.

Using Transfer Paper to Transfer Photos to Fabric

Photos can also be printed onto fabric using transfer paper (purchased at your local quilt shop), good-quality cotton fabric, and a hot iron.

Step 1:

Reduce or enlarge photo as needed for your particular project and print onto transfer paper following manufacturer's directions.

Step 2:

Trim off any excess paper from the edges of your photo.

Step 3:

Heat iron to cotton or linen setting. **Hint:** *For best results, use an iron without steam vents to ensure even transferring.*

Step 4:

Place cotton fabric right side up on a hard work surface such as a counter or solid table covered with a pad or heat-resistant cover. An ironing board could be too unstable. Place transfer face down onto pressed fabric aligning photo with grain of fabric. **Hint:** *Cover transfer with tissue before pressing to protect fabric from yellowing when exposed to hot iron.*

Step 5:

Place iron on top of the transfer and press down hard. Wait five or six seconds (depends upon temperature of iron) and move the iron to another section. Continue until the entire transfer has been set. Be sure to lift and move the iron, not push it across the transfer as that can cause shifting. **Hint:** *You may need to do a trial run to get the correct heat setting and length of heat time for your iron.*

Step 6:

Once you have heated the entire transfer, immediately remove the paper by pulling away with the grain of the fabric. Do not remove the transfer paper at a diagonal since that can cause distortion of image. **Hint:** *If the paper doesn't come off easily, re-iron the transfer and pull away while hot. If the transfer cools too much, it becomes difficult to remove.*

Making a Quilt

Sewing the Blocks Together

Once all of the blocks for your quilt have been made, place them on a flat surface such as a design wall or floor to decide on the best placement.

Sew the blocks together. You can do this by sewing the blocks in rows, then sewing the rows together; or, sew the blocks in pairs then sew pairs together. Continue sewing in pairs until entire quilt top is sewn together. (**Diagram 34**)

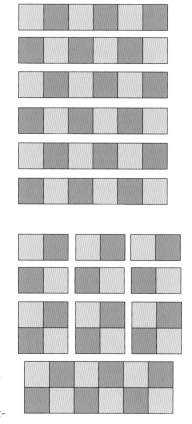

Adding Borders

Borders are usually added to a quilt sides first, then top and bottom.

Simple Borders

Step 1:

Measure the quilt top lengthwise and cut two border strips to that length by the width measurement given in the project instructions. Strips may have to be **34**

pieced to achieve the correct length. To make the joining seam less noticeable, sew the strips together diagonally. Place two strips right sides together at right angles. Sew a diagonal seam. (**Diagram 35**).

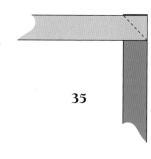

35

Step 2:

Trim excess fabric 1/4" from stitching. (**Diagram 36**)

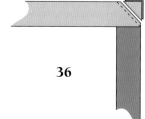

36

Step 3:

Press seam open. (**Diagram 37**)

Step 4:

Sew strips to the sides of the quilt. Now measure the quilt top crosswise, being sure to include the borders you have just added. Cut two border strips, following the width measurement given in the instructions.

Step 5:

Add these borders to the top and bottom of the quilt. Repeat this process for any additional borders. Use the 1/4" seam allowance at all times and press all of the seams to the darker side. Press the quilt top carefully.

Mitered Borders

Mitered borders are much more time-consuming, but sometimes the results may well be worth the effort.

37

Step 1:

Measure the quilt top lengthwise. Cut two strips that length plus twice the finished border width plus 1/2" for seam allowances. Piece if necessary referring to step 1 in Simple Borders above.

Step 2:

Measure the quilt top crosswise. Cut, piecing if necessary, two strips that length plus twice the finished border width plus 1/2".

Step 3:

Find the midpoint of border strip by folding strip in half. (**Diagram 38**).

Step 4:
Place strip right sides together with quilt top matching midpoint of border with midpoint of quilt side. Pin in place. (**Diagram 39**) Pin border to quilt top along entire side.

Step 5:
Beginning 1/4" from top edge, sew border strip to quilt top, ending 1/4" from bottom edge. Backstitch at beginning and ending of sewing. (**Diagram 40**)

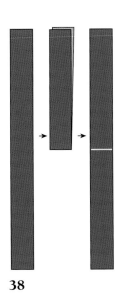

38

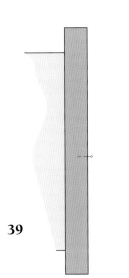

39

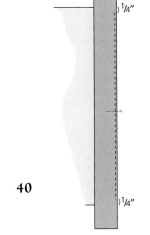

40

Step 6:
To finish corners, fold quilt top in half diagonally; borders will extend straight up and away from quilt. Place ruler along folded edge of quilt top going into border strip; draw a diagonal line on the border. (**Diagram 41**)

Step 7:
Beginning at corner of quilt top, stitch along drawn line to edge of border strip (**Diagram 42**)

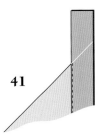

41

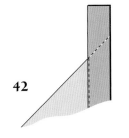

42

Step 8:
Open quilt at corner to check miter. If satisfied, trim excess fabric 1/4" from diagonal seam. (**Diagram 43**)

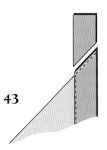

43

Step 9:
Repeat process at remaining three corners.

Finishing Your Quilt

Attaching the Batting and Backing

There are a number of different types of batting on the market today including the new fusible battings that eliminate the need for basting. Your choice of batting will depend upon how you are planning to use your quilt. If the quilt is to serve as a wall hanging, you will probably want to use a thin cotton batting. A quilt made with a thin cotton or cotton/polyester blend works best for machine quilting. Very thick polyester batting should be used only for tied quilts.

The best fabric for quilt backing is 100% cotton fabric. If your quilt is larger than the available fabric you will have to piece your backing fabric. When joining the fabric, try not to have a seam going down the center. Instead cut off the selvages and make a center strip that is about 36" wide and have narrower strips at the sides. Seam the pieces together and carefully press the seams open. (This is one of the few times in making a quilt that a seam should be pressed open.) Several fabric manufacturers are now selling fabric in 90" or 108"-widths for use as backing fabric.

It is a good idea to remove the batting from its wrapping 24 hours before you plan to use it and open it out to full size. You will find that the batting will now lie flat when you are ready to use it.

The batting and the backing should be cut about one to two inches larger on all sides than the quilt top. Place the backing wrong side up on a flat surface. Smooth out the batting on top of this, matching the outer edges. Center the quilt top, right side up, on top of the batting.

Now the quilt layers must be held together before quilting, and there are several methods for doing this:

Safety-pin Basting: Starting from the center and working toward the edges, pin through all layers at one time with large safety pins. The pins should be placed no more than 4" apart. As you work, think of your quilting plan to make sure that the pins will avoid prospective quilting lines.

Thread Basting: Baste the three layers together with long stitches. Start in the center and sew toward the edges in a number of diagonal lines.

Quilt-gun Basting: This handy trigger tool pushes nylon tags through all layers of the quilt. Start in the center and work toward the outside edges. The tags should be placed about 4" apart. You can sew right over the tags, which can then be easily removed by cutting them off with scissors.

Spray or Heat-Set Basting: Several manufacturers have spray adhesives available especially for quilters. Apply these products by following the manufacturer's directions. You might want to test these products before you use them to make sure that they meet your requirements.

Fusible Iron-on Batting: These battings are a wonderful new way to hold quilt layers together without using any of the other time-consuming methods of basting. Again, you will want to test these battings to be certain that you are happy with the results. Follow the manufacturer's directions.

Quilting

If you have never used a sewing machine for quilting, you may want to find a book and read about the technique. You do not need a special machine for quilting. Just make sure that your machine has been oiled and is in good working condition.

If you are going to do machine quilting, you should invest in an even-feed foot. This foot is designed to feed the top and bottom layers of a quilt evenly through the machine. The foot prevents puckers from forming as you machine quilt. Use a fine transparent nylon thread in the top and regular sewing thread in the bobbin.

Quilting in the ditch is one of the easiest ways to machine quilt.

This is a term used to describe stitching along the seam line between two pieces of fabric. Using your fingers, pull the blocks or pieces apart slightly and machine stitch right between the two pieces. The stitching will look better if you keep the stitching to the side of the seam that does not have the extra bulk of the seam allowance under it. The quilting will be hidden in the seam.

Free-form machine quilting can be used to quilt around a design or to quilt a motif. The quilting is done with a darning foot and the feed dogs down on the sewing machine. It takes practice to master Free-form quilting because you are controlling the movement of the quilt under the needle rather than the sewing machine moving the quilt. You can quilt in any direction—up and down, side-to-side and even in circles—without pivoting the quilt around the needle. Practice this quilting method before trying it on your quilt.

Attaching the Continuous Machine Binding

Once the quilt has been quilted, it must be bound to cover the raw edges.

Step 1:

Start by trimming the backing and batting even with the quilt top. Measure the quilt top and cut enough 2^1/$_2$" wide strips to go around all four sides of the quilt plus 12". Join the strips end to end with diagonal seams and trim the corners. Press the seams open. (**Diagram 44**)

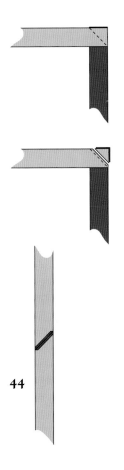

44

Step 2:

Cut one end of the strip at a 45-degree angle and press under ^{1}/$_4$". (**Diagram 45**)

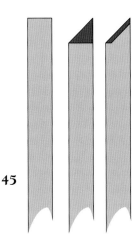

45

Step 3:

Press entire strip in half lengthwise, wrong sides together. (**Diagram 46**)

46

Step 4:

On the back of the quilt, position the binding in the middle of one side, keeping the raw edges together. Sew the binding to the quilt with the ^{1}/$_4$" seam allowance, beginning about three inches below the folded end of the binding. (**Diagram 47**) At the corner, stop ^{1}/$_4$" from the edge of the quilt and backstitch.

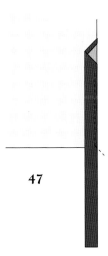

47

Step 4:
Fold binding away from quilt so it is at a right angle to edge just sewn. Then, fold the binding back on itself so the fold is on the quilt edge and the raw edges are aligned with the adjacent side of the quilt. Begin sewing at the quilt edge. (**Diagram 48**)

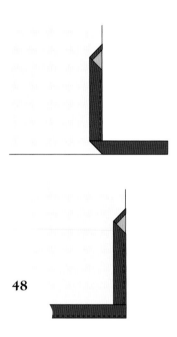

48

Step 5:
Continue in the same way around the remaining sides of the quilt. Stop about 2" away from the starting point. Trim any excess binding and tuck it inside the folded end. Finish the stitching. (**Diagram 49**)

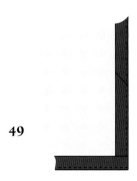

49

Step 6:
Fold the binding to the front of the quilt so the seam line is covered; machine-stitch the binding in place on the front of the quilt. Use a straight stitch or tiny zigzag with invisible or matching thread. If you have a sewing machine that does embroidery stitches, you may want to use your favorite stitch.

Adding a Rod Pocket
In order to hang your Time Capsule quilt for family and friends to enjoy, you will need to attach a rod pocket to the back.

Step 1:
Cut a strip of fabric, 6" wide by the width of the quilt.

Step 2:
Fold short ends of strip under 1/4", then fold another 1/4". Sew along first fold. (**Diagram 50**)

50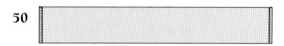

Step 3:
Fold strip lengthwise with wrong sides together. Sew along raw edges with a 1/4" seam allowance to form a long tube. (**Diagram 51**)

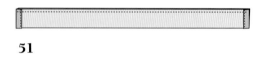

51

Step 4:
Place tube on ironing surface with seam up and centered; press seam open and folds flat. (**Diagram 52**)

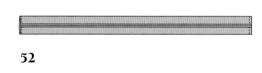

52

Step 5:
Place tube on back of quilt, seam side against quilt, about 1" from top edge and equal distant from side edges. (**Diagram 53**) Pin in place so tube is straight across quilt.

Step 6:

Hand stitch top and bottom edges of tube to back of quilt being careful not to let stitches show on front of quilt.

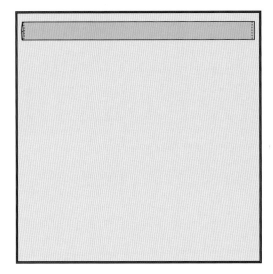

53

Labeling Your Quilt

Always sign and date your quilt when finished. You can make a label by cross-stitching or embroidering or even writing on a label with a permanent marking pen on the back of your quilt. If you are friends with your computer, you can even create an attractive label on the computer.

Metric Equivalents

inches	cm	inches	cm	inches	cm
1	2.54	11	27.94	21	53.34
2	5.08	12	30.48	22	55.88
3	7.62	13	33.02	23	58.42
4	10.16	14	35.56	24	60.96
5	12.70	15	38.10	30	76.20
6	15.24	16	40.64	36	91.44
7	17.78	17	43.18	42	106.68
8	20.32	18	45.72	48	121.92
9	22.86	19	48.26	54	137.16
10	25.40	20	50.8	60	152.40

Index

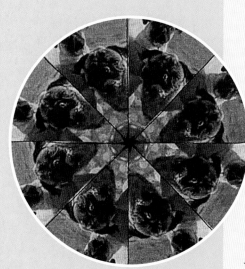